DARK LORE

DAILY GRAIL PUBLISHING

Darklore Volume 8
Copyright © 2014 by Greg Taylor (Editor)

ISBN: 978-0-9874224-6-0

Daily Grail Publishing
Brisbane, Australia
userhelp@dailygrail.com
www.dailygrail.com

Contents

"You are an explorer, and you represent our species, and the greatest good you can do is to bring back a new idea, because our world is endangered by the absence of good ideas. Our world is in crisis because of the absence of consciousness."

- Terence McKenna

If you would like to be notified of future releases of *Darklore*, please send an email to darklore@dailygrail.com. Please be assured your contact details will not be used for any other purpose.

EDITOR'S INTRODUCTION

"**W**e used to look up in the sky and wonder at our place in the stars. Now we just look down and worry about our place in the dirt". So says Matthew McConaughey's character in the upcoming science fiction film from director Christopher Nolan, *Interstellar*. As someone who was born in the immediate year after humanity's first touch of the lunar surface, this line resonates powerfully; I grew up dreaming of how far into space – and in how many numbers – we would have ventured by the time I had children of my own. That dream turned out to be a chimera, as in the four decades since Apollo 17 humans have barely slipped beyond the Earth's atmosphere – a lone thousandth of the distance that the Apollo crews dared to cross.

There are very good reasons why this has happened. As it turns out, humans aren't particularly well-built for traveling through space; we are biologically designed to work best in a gravity well, shielded from cosmic radiation by the magnetosphere of our mother planet. Any voyages beyond the Moon – a mere 3 days of travel to achieve orbit, compared to 5-10 *months* if we traveled to our nearest neighbour Mars – would entail major dangers to the health of the astronauts, and seemingly impossible logistics of how to get back off that planet once there…after all, Mars has a lot more gravity than the Moon.

But designing a way of escaping the significant gravitational influence of our own planet was once deemed near-impossible also, and we quickly overcame that hurdle once we set our mind to it. I don't think we lack for the ingenuity to solve the problems involved in space travel; rather, we now lack the courage. The early astronauts were willing to strap themselves into a tin-can atop a mountain of fuel and ignite it, putting their trust in neophyte astro-maths and physics geeks to do the sums well enough that they weren't hurled into the depths of space for eternity. Today, to lose one astronaut would shut down a space program for months – perhaps years – whilst blame was apportioned and new risk assessments performed, in order to ensure the safety of those that followed.

But space travel *is* risky. When the great age of exploration of our own planet took place, ships sank, explorers were killed by unwelcoming indigenous inhabitants, and travelers were at times stranded in new and exotic locations awaiting rescue. Risk assessments weren't performed, ships weren't docked until a better, unsinkable boat was designed. Exploring new ground isn't for the faint-hearted, it's for the bold and curious who are willing to risk their safety to be the first beyond the threshold.

Similarly, though perhaps not on such a grand scale, the exploration of the lands that lie beyond the borders of our knowledge – and that includes, at times, the mythical lands that turn out not to exist after all – demands a personality that is willing to leap outside of the comfort zone, to step upon the unstable grounds of untested ontologies, and brave the taunts of those who mistake the ventures of the supremely curious for the dazed wandering of a lost soul.

The anthology series you are currently reading is dedicated to serving the needs of such explorers. I hope the current volume takes you into waters previously uncharted, and planets undiscovered.

Awake

A history of sane hallucinations

by *Mike Jay*

n February 1758 the 90-year-old Charles Lullin, a retired Swiss civil servant whose sight had been progressively failing since a cataract operation five years before, began to see considerably more than he had become accustomed to. For the next several months he was visited in his apartment by a silent procession of figures, invisible to everyone but him: young men in magnificent cloaks, perfectly coiffured ladies carrying boxes on their heads, girls dancing in silks and ribbons. These visions were recorded and published in 1760 by his grandson, the naturalist Charles Bonnet, after whom the syndrome of hallucinations in the elderly and partially sighted would much later be named.

This celebrated case is one of the founding studies in the science of hallucinations, and frames the subject in distinctive ways. Most significantly, it has no link with mental illness: Lullin's eyesight may have dimmed but his cognitive faculties were perfectly sharp, and he had no difficulty recognising his hallucinations as unreal. His experience was clearly different in kind from those experienced in psychoses such as schizophrenia: rather, it highlights the remarkable range of organic conditions, from neurological disorders to drug effects, that produce 'hallucinations in the sane'.

Much has been learned in the intervening century about the brain states and optical processes that lie behind such experiences, but the old question remains: what, if anything, do such hallucinations have to tell us? They cannot be dismissed as symptoms of insanity, and nor are they purely random sensory data: on the contrary, their content is curiously consistent. Miniature people, for example, are a common sight for those with Charles Bonnet syndrome: Oliver Sacks recalls a patient who was accompanied for a couple of weeks by "little people a few inches high, like elves or fairies, with little green caps, climbing up the sides of her wheelchair".[1] These little folk are also witnessed in many other circumstances: by sufferers from migraine, epilepsy or Parkinson's disease, those on mind-altering drugs such as DMT (dimethyltryptamine) or magic mushrooms, or in withdrawal from alcohol or sedatives. These are wildly different causes, but the miniature people they generate are strikingly similar. They share many curious but consistent qualities: a tendency to appear in groups, for example, or arrayed in phalanxes ('numerosity'), to wear headgear or exotic dress, and to go about their business autonomously, paying no attention to the subject's attempts to interact with them. Who are these little people? Do they have a message for us? And if not, what is the meaning of their insistent qualities?

From the perspective of the neurosciences, such hallucinatory stereotypes are privileged, if cryptic, glimpses into the deep

structure of the brain: the fact that they can be generated by so many unrelated causes suggests hardwired perceptual structures that reliably manufacture them. But they also have a cultural life – and, for quintessentially private mental events, a remarkably well-defined social history. They are assigned distinct meanings in different cultures: in many, their familiar appearance is taken as evidence not of their neurological basis but of their independent existence in a transpersonal or spirit world. The phenomenon appears to be consistent through history – the oldest example typically cited in the literature is the 'little strangers' who appeared to St Macarius the Elder in his desert solitude around 350 CE – but susceptible to varied cultural interpretations: in Ireland such figures might be described as leprechauns, in Norway as trolls and so on. Do these archetypes draw on a private but universal mental landscape? If so, we might square the circle of nature and culture with the suggestion that they have a basis in neurology but their interpretation shifts with the times: the fairies of old now manifesting more commonly as aliens.

In western cultures these folkloric entities have been elaborated into cultural and literary forms, and indeed have been adopted as clinical labels. One of the many terms for seeing miniature people is 'Lilliput sight', another is 'Alice in Wonderland syndrome'; naturally it has been suggested that Jonathan Swift may have experienced it during his demented final years, while Charles Dodgson may have based Alice's distortions of scale on an account of mushroom-eating Siberian shamans in Mordecai Cooke's drug compendium, *Seven Sisters of Sleep* (1860). Their classic manifestations in our culture, from traditional tales of fairy rings and hollow hills through to literary renderings such as Christina Rosetti's *Goblin Market*, include the message that they are alluring but also mischievous and deceitful: those to whom they appear must beware of tricks, and of being lured into magical scenes that dissolve into cruel traps. Does this consensus mean that these entities – djinn, sprites, elves – really exist, or in

some way inhabit the borders of our collective consciousness? Or does it warn that the attempt to extract meaning or profit from such encounters is a fool's quest?

A Soul Adrift

If hallucinations are subject to cultural influence, the most significant of the modern era is probably the word itself. 'Hallucination' is a term of surprisingly recent coinage, adopted in 1817 by the French alienist Jean-Etienne Dominique Esquirol.

Esquirol's stated goals were relatively modest. He wanted to create a single category for all sense disturbances: previous terms such as 'vision', 'apparition' or 'spectral illusion' were all weighted towards the visual, and he needed a term that applied equally to hearing voices or feeling the sensation of bugs under the skin. He also wanted to reflect what he conceived as a primary distinction between misperceptions, which he termed 'illusions', and perceptions constructed entirely by the mind. Interpreting a fleeting shadow as a person or hearing a voice in a babbling stream are illusions; but "if a man has the intimate conviction of actually perceiving a sensation for which there is no external object, he is in a hallucinatory state; he is a visionary" (*visionnaire*).[2] Hallucinations, like dreams, are independent of the senses: those who experience them might be said to be 'dreaming while awake'.

Esquirol's description of the hallucinator as a 'visionary' sounds strange to modern ears precisely because his new label transformed its object so profoundly. Private sensory events (to adopt a neutral term, though one that fails to distinguish hallucinations from dreams) have been integrated into the public sphere throughout human history, and often as legitimate sources of information: oracles, messages from ancestors or the voice of God. The word that Esquirol repurposed, *alucinari*, had signified a wandering in mind, a soul adrift: Dante, most famously, used it to describe the effects of the siren song on Odysseus. But from the late 1830s, when 'hallucination' penetrated first clinical and then common language, it cast a medical shadow over the borderlands previously claimed by 'soul' and 'spirit'. The ambiguities present in terms such as 'visionary' were overwritten with an implicit judgment that these were not messages from beyond the self but errors in mental functioning. As such they were by definition pathological, and increasingly viewed as symptoms of insanity.

Debates in mid-century French psychiatry reflected these assumptions. Were hallucinations a malfunction of the sense organs or, as Esquirol maintained, a "central" phenomenon of the brain itself? Was it possible for them to co-exist with reason? Should all mystic states be regarded as hallucinations? Such questions were put to the test by Esquirol's protégé Jacques-Joseph Moreau de Tours, who experimented with large doses of hashish in the company of a literary demi-monde that included Théophile Gautier, Gérard de Nerval and Charles Baudelaire. He concluded that, even at the mindbending peak of its effects, hashish produced only illusions based on sensory distortion rather than 'true hallucinations', manufactured by the mind from whole cloth. "A hallucination", he wrote in 1845, "is the most frequent symptom and the fundamental fact of delirium, mental illness and madness".[3] The physician and theorist of dreams Alfred Maury assumed a direct equivalence between hallucinators and the insane: "for what are the latter, if not minds who believe in their hallucinations as if they were serious facts?"[4]

As visionary experience was drawn into the ambit of medicine, it became less visible in normal life. 'Retrospective medicine', a term coined in 1869 by the physician and positivist philosopher Emile Littré, set about diagnosing Moses, Socrates and Muhammad as epileptics, hysterics or paranoiacs. Anomalous private experiences, now that they carried the taint of insanity, were less commonly shared. For example, the mysterious phenomenon of pain from amputated limbs had been anecdotally familiar at least since it was described in Descartes' *Meditations*; but before the American neurologist Silas Weir Mitchell could offer the first full account of 'phantom limb syndrome' in 1872, he had been obliged to spend many years delicately eliciting case histories from invalid soldiers who had kept their strange sensations to themselves for fear of being transferred to an asylum.

It was against this background that the Society of Psychical Research (SPR) in 1889 launched an 'International Census of Waking Hallucinations in the Sane'. British doctors and philosophers had amassed many vivid reports of 'apparitions' and 'spectral illusions' in the early decades of the nineteenth century, and disputed whether they were ghosts, sensory errors or mental derangements; after mid-century, the term 'hallucination' had brought with it a markedly more clinical and admonitory tone. Henry Maudsley, in *Hallucinations of the Senses* (1878), diagnosed Joan of Arc with religious mania, characterised such visionary episodes as "discordant notes in the grand harmony" of human nature, and cautioned the reader to "guard against" them by "prudent care of the body and wise culture of the mind".[5]

The president of the SPR was the Cambridge philosophy professor Henry Sidgwick, who set out the aims and results of the census in a series of public addresses that aimed to reclaim hallucinations for sanity, but struggled with the trap set by the word itself. He recognised that it implied at best "erroneous and illusory belief", at worst something "entirely false and morbid", but he could offer no viable alternative: partly on Esquirol's grounds that he wished to include voice-hearing and invisible touches along with visions, but also because he was determined to avoid any term that might imply belief in the supernatural and thereby exclude sceptics from his sample. His final wording skirted the problem, inquiring whether the subject has ever had "a vivid impression of seeing or being touched by a living being or inanimate object, or of hearing a voice, which impression, so far as you could discover, was not due to an external physical cause". 'Hallucination' was, however, included in the 'Instructions to Collectors' on the back of the form as "in many cases ... the only proper term".[6]

The census was distributed through the SPR's network of seven hundred members, and aimed for 35,000 respondents; in the end it

managed 6481, with 727 positive replies to its question, suggesting
that these 'vivid impressions' were familiar to around 11 per cent
of the sane population. But what did they mean? Despite his care
to alienate neither spiritualists nor materialists, Sidgwick was
considerably closer to the former: his academic and public work
sought to reconcile science, religion and ethics, and he argued that
a moral order could only exist if some part of human personality
survived bodily death. The census was part of a wide-ranging
programme of research into telepathy and thought transference,
and his overriding interest in the data was as suggestive evidence
for the reality of these powers, as well as for life after death. The
first case he quotes is that of "a figure in a brown dress with broad
lace collar and golden hair"[7] seen by three persons on separate
occasions; he is most excited by cases of 'collective hallucination',
which are methodically parsed for logical explanation: coincidence,
telepathy or supernatural agency?

Sidgwick decoupled hallucinations from pathology and insanity,
but he still treated them as evidence of something else rather than
as phenomena that might have meaning in their own right. This
assumption was clearly shared by most of the census subjects: their
'vivid impressions' are almost all of people or obliquely human
forms, typically departed relatives or mysterious figures in black,
materialising and vanishing in the manner of the ghost stories of
the time. If nothing else, the census reveals that the private world
of hallucinations can be dated as easily as fashion or literature.
Fascinating on many levels (as a precursor of Mass-Observation, or
a spectral outline of the late Victorian psyche), the SPR's initiative
failed to generate a convincing panorama, or even a snapshot, of the
reality that its members hoped to bring into the purview of science.
Hallucinations might not be a sign of madness, but neither could
they be shown to convey any clear message or evidence of a world
beyond themselves.

True Hallucinations?

During the twentieth century hallucinations were reclaimed by a medical science that (at least after Pierre Janet and Sigmund Freud's work on hypnosis) was less interested in their content than in the biological mechanisms that underpinned them. Such mechanisms had long been inferred, and occasionally glimpsed. On a stroll through town one day in 1758, Charles Lullin had stopped to peer at a giant scaffold tower; when he returned home he found it sitting in miniature form in his living room. This prompted him to experiment with the blue square that often rippled across his vision: he found that if he saw it next to a fountain in the distance it appeared to be the size of a blanket, but as he focused on closer objects it shrank to the size of a handkerchief.

More recent studies have suggested that Lilliputian sight may be related to disturbance of the 'size constancy' function in the visual association cortex, which allows us to recognise automatically that an object is not actually shrinking as it recedes from view. Today's leading researchers in the field are beginning to tease apart the different brain regions and neurochemical pathways involved and to associate particular visual forms with each. Dominic ffytche's work, to take one example, also suggests that Charles Bonnet syndrome is itself a chimera: since its identification in 1936 it has blurred the boundaries between eye disease and senility, but now it seems to be splitting into two or more quite separate conditions.[8] And as these deep mechanisms are being exposed, such cracks are spreading: is 'hallucination' a meaningful category at all, or simply a ragbag of poorly understood symptoms with causes as disparate as macular degeneration, the prelude to an epileptic seizure, the effects of withdrawal from alcohol, or voices heard while drifting off to sleep?

If the category is dissolving under scrutiny, the ideological power of the label remains nonetheless intact. The definition of 'hallucination' in the American Psychiatric Association's *Diagnostic and Statistical Manual of Mental Disorders* (DSM-IV) is still Esquirol's: "a sensory perception that has the compelling sense of reality of a true perception but that occurs without external stimulation of the relevant sensory organ". It is impossible within this framework to investigate whether private perceptions might be objectively real, and the twentieth-century counterparts of the SPR operated at the margins of science. Prominent among them were drug experimenters such as the renegade neuroscientist John Lilly, who postulated an 11-level model of the mind to explain how his experiments with LSD in sensory deprivation tanks might have plugged him into a cosmic computer, and the psychedelic explorer Terence McKenna, whose DMT and mushroom revelations – described in his book *True Hallucinations* (1993) and elsewhere – were mediated by Lilliputian folk he described as "self-transforming machine elves".

McKenna's elves (or gnomes, as he sometimes called them) have become the paradigm for the little people encountered in drug-induced hallucinations, and the focus for debates about their ontological status and meaning. McKenna insisted they were "transhuman, hyperdimensional and extremely alien", and that they had a vital message for humanity. As with the SPR, however, the content of the message was less memorable than the messengers. McKenna's elves blew his mind while urgently instructing him to remain rational ("Don't give in to astonishment! Pay attention to what we're doing!")[9] but the most coherent revelation he was able to extract from them was that "some enormously reality-rearranging thing"[10] was due to take place around 21 December 2012.

McKenna recognized that his elves partook of the little people's trickster archetype, but he was less ready to acknowledge that such entities are also regularly generated by more mundane stimuli such as migraines and Parkinson's medications. For him they were the ultimate other, self-evidently beyond anything the human mind could conjure unassisted; their irreducible strangeness was proof of

their transhuman status. Yet they have clear commonalities with the visions generated by less exotic causes, which indeed might provide clues to their meaning. 'Lilliputian hallucinations' tend to be confidently oblivious of the real world, marching and clambering round the observer while ignoring any attempts to communicate with them. Perhaps the mischievous and mysterious nature of entities encountered on psychedelics reflects a tension between two different aspects of the experience: on the one hand an overwhelming sense of immanence and cosmic revelation, on the other an inscrutable scene that is uninterested in the consciousness that is generating it. In this interpretation, the message of the elves might indeed be a profound one: just because this is all happening in your head, it doesn't mean that it's all about you.

Drug-induced hallucinations can of course be taken seriously without being taken literally. Oliver Sacks's experiences, recounted in his recent book on hallucinations, offer a fine example. Adhering to Moreau de Tours' distinction with hashish, Sacks mentions but doesn't describe his experience on classic psychedelics such as LSD and mescaline, which might be better categorised as 'illusogens' than hallucinogens. Instead, he concentrates on full-scale deliriants such as a massive dose of the Parkinson's medication Artane: a substance that, emerging from the profane world of pharmacy, lacks the sacred resonances of mushrooms or DMT. His reports make no claim to objective veracity, but they also resist easy reduction to symptoms of neurological impairment. They are related candidly, as lucid and plausible as reality itself: when he sees and hears his parents descending into his garden from a helicopter, he feels nothing but surprise and delight; when they abruptly vanish, "the silence and emptiness, the disappointment, reduced me to tears".[11]

Such experiences may amount to no more than neurological flotsam, but they cannot be willed away: they must be dealt with as if real, just as Charles Bonnet or Parkinson's sufferers must learn to cope with the persistent and ultimately banal presence of their tiny companions. They are evidence neither of insanity nor of the spirit world: the challenge is to assimilate them into the rest of our mental life. What hallucinations have to tell us might be that the inner workings of our senses are a riotous carnival, driven by an engine of unimaginable processing power whose most spectacular illusion is reality itself.

Mike Jay is the author of *Emperors of Dreams: Drugs in the Nineteenth Century*. His most recent book, *The Influencing Machine*, is now available in the US under the title *A Visionary Madness*.

a social history of
BALL
LIGHTNING

The chimera that came in from the cold

by *Martin Shough*

ack in 1967 the astronomer Gerard Kuiper dismissed a 10% residue of unexplained UFO reports with a wave of the hand, thinking it "reasonable to assume" that this testimony must be "so distorted or incomplete as to defy all analysis." However, he advocated a major Defence Department/FAA programme to research "very rare natural phenomena" such as ball lightning. Why? Because "no adequate data yet exist of ball lightning", even though its existence had been "known for at least a century".[1]

This raises a very interesting question: How was it possible for science to "know" anything with "no adequate data"? The answer is that science did *not* know. Rather, ball lightning had been kept in the natural philospher's cabinet of curiosities along with a jumble of Forteana such as sea serpents, will-o'-the-wisps, fabulous mirages and spirits of the dead for a couple of hundred years. Disbelief and credulity swirled around together in a miasma of hopeless speculation until, during the early 20th century, the authoritative consensus settled into scepticism - a position which had only quite recently begun to change at the time Kuiper was writing.

Unpicking some of the reason and unreason behind this curious condition of scientific double-think is instructive. Logically and evidentially speaking, there is precious little difference between a "very rare natural phenomenon" which is unexplained and an unexplained phenomenon characterised as a "UFO". Even more subtle is the distinction sometimes drawn between "a unique natural phenomenon never before observed" and a UFO. There will always be unique combinations of natural phenomena never before observed (in practice), so how is a distinction to be supported between such effects and UFOs? Is there a real epistemological distinction? Or is it mere semantics?

The difference appears in practice to arise because there are two levels of "explanation" whose meanings are weighted differently in the two cases: There is a level of detailed physical understanding, i.e. a link-by-link chain of observed processes accurately modelled in theory; and there is a level of conceptual classification. When either of these levels is satisfied we experience a sense of accounting, and when both are satisfied there is a closure which we experience as "explanation".

Neither in the case of "unknown natural phenomenon" nor in the case of "unidentified flying object" is the level of detailed physical understanding satisfied, by definition; the difference enters in the conceptual classification and has to do almost exclusively with the way these ideas are emotionally connoted. Specifically, it is the mechanistic aura of the former and the animistic aura of the latter that sets them apart. The history of science associates mechanistic models with productive explanations, animistic models with backward-looking resistance to explanations. The extraterrestrial hypothesis (ETH) and its analogues are for practical purposes regarded as examples of relict primitive animism.

Ball lightning emerges with some sense of explanation out of the primary category of "rare and unexplained phenomena" to the extent that it replaces (these days) animistic with mechanistic connotations. The collective term is emotionally neutral, the terms "ball lightning" and "UFO" are not individually so, and parity is broken; a coupled particle-pair of overall neutral charge is, so to speak, dissociated into two particles of opposite charge which fly in different directions in the social field potential. The positive "ball lightning" particle is eventually scavenged by surrounding atoms of incomplete theory; the "UFO" particle is left to wander, a free negative ion in a lonely search for an appropriate theory with which to recombine. It is a pragmatic fact, quite separate from the question of evidence, that an animistically connoted interpretation is not supported by the usual social-institutional legitimations of science as a valid "explanation".

It was also in 1967 that the distinguished British physicist and erstwhile intelligence mandarin R. V. Jones opined that most witnesses in UFO cases which could not be explained had probably made "substantial errors", and that "flying saucers" were therefore almost certainly a fantasy; whereas this same corpus of substantial errors allowed Jones to conclude that "an as yet unrecognised natural phenomenon" was "distinctly possible". In illustration of this he noted that ball lightning "has long been both asserted and disputed" and could perhaps be a similar sort of case. But he objected that unexplained UFO cases, in contradistinction to ball lightning, were never reported by scientifically trained observers, finally declaring that "little short of a tangible relic would dispel my scepticism of flying saucers".[2] The error of fact here (many still-unexplained UFO reports have been made by scientifically trained, indeed scientifically illustrious, observers) seems almost negligible beside the tangle of category mistakes, non sequiturs and imported assumptions in which it is embedded.

Exactly similar objections continue to be heard regularly in the 21st century, and it is fascinating to be able to record that it has all been said before. Respected authorities such as Humphreys, Hagenguth and Berger in the 1930s, 1940s, 1950s and even into the 1960s regularly dismissed ball lightning in much the same language. So how did ball lightning come to survive and flourish as a scientific topic in the absence of a "tangible relic"?

Photographs and films were refuted by these sceptics as hoaxes, lens flares, streetlights, fireworks and so forth; eyewitnesses were regarded as an unreliable source of data, and were said to have misreported ordinary lightning, burning debris or retinal after-images; reports of burns and damage were said to be due to ordinary lightning strikes, unrelated fires or hoaxes; there were no concrete data in new reports and "fantastic stories from the past" were hardly

scientific evidence; reports rarely seemed to be made by scientifically trained observers, instead they seemed more often to be made by peasants, labourers and other credulous laypersons; lightning experts declared that their long surveys with panoramic cameras had never so much as caught a glimpse of anything like ball lightning; and anyway, darting, drifting spheres of light were physically impossible, as no small volume of atmospheric gases could sustain the reported energies of the balls for even a moment by combustion, let alone move around for many seconds or even minutes against the wind, pass down chimneys and squeeze through keyholes. In short the authoritatively sanctioned view, shared by the dominant majority, was that the whole thing was utter nonsense, belonging with tales of sulphurous demons and sea serpents.

LIGHTNING IN A BOTTLE

Then along came the early days of research into nuclear fusion, and the concept of electromagnetic containment of hot plasmas. Lightning channels were such plasmas, confined in one dimension: could stable plasmas, confined in three dimensions, form in nature? The idea was no more than an analogy, but one which prompted a few physicists to look again at the reports. It turned out that self-confinement in the free atmosphere by means of electromagnetic forces alone would not work, and realistic energy densities could not be found; but it was a start, and gradually more people began to talk as though the stories were not quite so wild after all.

Perhaps, suggested Peter Kapitza in 1955, such a plasma could be externally fed by the energy of intense, high-frequency radio fields associated with storms? No such radio fields were discovered, and calculations showed that the energies available would be too small to support a lightning ball in this way, but the principle was a breakthrough. There were still no unimpeachable films, photographs or instrumental data; no "baby Kugelblitz" had been captured and analysed. But suddenly it was no longer preposterous to think of lightning balls floating down chimneys to terrorise people in their kitchens, for example, because the radio energy sustaining the ball would tend to be ducted as in a wave-guide.

At about this time military scientists began to conceive the idea of an energy weapon based on plasmoid projectiles, synthetic thunderbolts which would be capable of vapourizing the toughest armour, and research began during the next few years to generate controlled "lightning" balls in the laboratory. By the early nineteen-sixties, the Berkeley Radiation Laboratory of the University of California had developed a prototype plasma-weapon that expelled annular deuterium plasmoids at impressive velocity. It was thought that military applications of such weapons might be found in space, either in 'killer' satellites for disabling the new generation of spy satellites or as defences against ICBMs. The US Air Force Office of Scientific Research (AFOSR) began funding expensive secret programmes which were mirrored by similar efforts in the Soviet Union.

Meanwhile other theories of natural ball lightning came and went, such as cosmic rays focussed by the electric fields in thunderclouds. There was a quantum mechanical model involving a cold, dense electron gas self-confined by exchange forces, and even one which proposed spontaneous thermonuclear reactions: An unsuccessful, but nonetheless remarkable, efflorescence of ingenuity springing from what until recently had been (and to some still was) so much mere "humbug". Slowly the barometer of professional opinion continued to swing, so that despite a notable paucity of concrete evidence and an observational database inevitably corrupted by misinterpretations, hoaxes and old-wives' tales, the once-derided ball lightning began to exist, in the very practical sense that there was a widespread and growing consensus. At last scientists could start doing science.

Then in 1964, working on a grant from AFOSR administered through the Air Force Cambridge Research Laboratories (AFCRL), two physicists at Yeshiva University in New York built on Kapitza's idea and came up with the first nearly-workable theory based on dielectric inhomogeneities in DC electrical fields which remained the basis of further developments for many years. Now, thanks to the thirst for militarily useful ideas and the efforts of Finkelstein and Rubenstein, it was possible to give mathematical form to a model which explained many of the shapes, colours, movements, odours, noises, temperatures and durations which had been reported and scorned for generations.

Spheroidal and ellipsoidal forms turned out to be the only stable solutions of the field equation. These plasma forms could also be shown to behave somewhat like elastic solids, which explained the oft-reported "bouncing" motion of lightning balls. Later refinements based on low frequency AC. fields, such as had been observed in association with lightning, were developed by Edmond Dewan and others working at AFCRL.[3] This explained the reported persistence of ball lightning indoors by getting round the problem that in DC fields even non-metallic building structures tended to behave like conductive Faraday cages. The fit between theory and observation was improving, and although a completely satisfactory theory remained (and still remains) to be worked out, it was at last permissible for lightning balls to behave somewhat as, in fact, they had always behaved: bouncing, swooping, hovering, "investigating" chimneys and rooms, "pursuing" objects and people, sneaking through windows, keyholes and drainpipes.

By this time many physicists had begun exercising some creative hindsight, and history, as always, was written by the victors. Ball lightning began to be cited as the sort of novel phenomenon that objective science was always ready to embrace, provided only that there was good, reliable evidence. One began to hear about the fine qualifications of witnesses who had previously been ignored and derided.

In 1967 R.V. Jones was now able to point out that ball lightning had been reported by no less an observer than a former Deputy Director of the UK Meteorological Office, although the worthy Mr. Durward's two separate experiences with ball lightning back in 1934 and 1938 had singularly failed to impress the scientific world at the time, and years later had been dismissed by Swiss lightning expert K. Berger as one of those unevaluable "fantastic stories from the past".[4]

University of California physicist Leonard Loeb now felt secure enough to pronounce that lightning balls "have been too often seen and described by competent observers to be classed with flying saucers. They are not illusions".[5] And aviation journalist Philip Klass confidently explained in articles in 1966,[6,7] and in a book two years later,[8] that many puzzling reports of so-called UFOs could in fact now be explained as ball lightning.

Besides having unimpeachable witnesses, ball lightning could boast quantitative data, too. Back in 1936 a Mr. W. Morris, a resident of Dorstone, near Ross-on-Wye, Herefordshire, reported that a fireball "the size of a large orange" had descended into his water butt, which he said had contained "about four gallons of water". The water boiled for "several minutes" and even after twenty minutes was too hot to touch. Few people took much notice of Mr. Morris in 1936, but this feast of observational data has been richly savoured in more recent years.

In 1966 the University of Colorado was famously contracted by the US Air Force to assemble a report which would be a grand epitaph to its 20-year role as UFO report collection centre for the American public, a study known as the Condon Report. Not surprisingly ball lightning made its appearance therein and Mr. Morris's immortal fame was once more celebrated.

Martin D. Altschuler, a solar physicist then working at the National Center for Atmospheric Research, prefaced his discussion of UFOs and atmospheric electricity in the Condon Report by noting that ball lightning "although witnessed and reported many times in the

A contemporary woodcut of the 'Great Thunderstorm' at Widecombe in 1638, when an 8-foot ball of fire was described as striking and entering the church, killing four people.

past, has only with difficulty been established as a genuine scientific problem. Years of patient effort," explained Altschuler, "were required to distinguish ball lightning from retinal after-images and optical illusions." One may doubt that the witnesses, after years of thankless reporting, would much appreciate the "effort" of science in this regard. But Altschuler and many others have certainly appreciated the world-famous rain barrel anecdote of Mr. Morris.

Describing this antique story as a "singular" piece of evidence upon which much research has focused, Altschuler proceeded to assume that the initial water temperature in Mr. Morris's barrel was 20°C, that 1 litre of water evaporated from the barrel, and that the remaining 17 litres was raised to 90°C, concluding that a plasma 10 cm in diameter must have had an energy density of 5×10^9 joule/m^3, an order of magnitude greater than the energy density of an equivalent volume of singly-ionised air. Much depends, said Altschuler, on reliable energy estimates of such fireballs, and although these data have serious implications for some theories of ball lightning formation there are sufficient well-documented reports implying very high energy densities to "make the water barrel report very believable".[9]

It may be doubted whether water standing outside in a barrel in Herefordshire in October would be at 20°C, but never mind; one is impressed by how much may be inferred from so little, and is led to wonder in turn why, so consistently, nothing whatsoever can be inferred from reports of other aerial phenomena currently languishing in the holding category of "unidentified flying objects".

The Condon Report stopped thinking about any such story once it became evident that it could not be explained, typically appending the conclusion that it "cannot be verified or refuted" or that the lack of tangible evidence rendered it "of no probative value". This had been the extent of scientific ingenuity for twenty years and was plainly less than helpful. True, certain promising unknowns were considered at a special conference of atmospheric and plasma physicists to see if they had any relevance to the study of ball lightning and related phenomena. The general conclusion was that they probably did not, which appeared to put a stop to curiosity. "All participants agreed," reported Altschuler, "that the UFO cases presented contained insufficient data for a definitive scientific conclusion." End of story. Oh, but Altschuler encouraged people to write or 'phone in with any sightings of ball lightning.

"The size of an orange"? "Several minutes"? Surely we can do better than this. The amount of latent information in many still-unexplained UFO reports is potentially enormous by comparison. Perhaps some of the phenomena would turn out to be relatives of ball lightning, and perhaps some would not, but certainly we will never know if we exert disproportionate negative pressure on efforts to find out.

The Condon Report made space for Gerard Kuiper to peer down his nose at "this odd and discouraging assemblage of data", an ill-perfumed rabble beside the seemly decorum of ball lightning reports; and made space for R. V. Jones to perpetuate the dual myth that ball lightning gained scientific opprobrium due to reports from trained observers, whereas "flying saucers" were sadly less fortunate in being so often sponsored by hoaxers, liars, the deranged and the merely dull, never by wholly reliable people. Of course, added Jones as a rider, it was quite possible that the tiny residue of unexplained UFO reports from those few who were somewhat less dull could easily have been . . . you guessed it, misinterpretations of ball lightning.

RADAR-REFLECTIVE SOMETHINGS

Now whilst every conscientious sceptical investigator would recognise that there are some intriguing reports among that fluctuating residue of unknowns that represents the "evidence for unidentified flying objects", and would agree that we must allow the possibility that remarkable phenomena are observed, nevertheless he or she might feel that "intriguing" was slim evidence on which to found an animistic theory of extraterrestrial incursions. This is a very honourable position to take. But it is a difficult position to maintain, under tension between the opposite lazy equilibria of "debunking" and "believing".

Consider as an apt example the Lakenheath-Bentwaters case of 1956 – itself brought to light in the Condon Report – which did much to alter the complexion of the UFO debate during the 1970s and 1980s with its compelling mix of multiple radar and visual detections, by both USAF ground observers and RAF interceptor jets, all wrapped up in official telex reports from impressed intelligence officers on the spot.[10] It remains a fascinating microcosm of the whole debate more than half a century after the first investigations, confusing but still unresolved despite a considerable amount of new information. By this I mean, of course, that it isn't resolved either as a simple and well-understood event or as a spaceship. The most one ought to say about this case is that radar-reflective somethings in the atmosphere possibly behaved in ways that stretch the theories developed to explain other radar-reflective somethings in the atmosphere. That isn't to say much. For most people it isn't enough. And because the information needed to explain in terms of link-by-link physical processes is lacking we tend to skip to the explanation-level of conceptual classification.

On this level the issues become cathected and significant, primitively polarised between mechanistic and animistic tendencies, and here the psychological desire for closure pulls us in the direction of incredulity or of credulity. Some give in to their sense of wonder, others to their sense of disgust. If it were a report of ball lightning everyone can see that the debate would have a wholly different complexion: Enchantment would not be embattled with its self-generated alter ego Disenchantment. The problem would be able to remain on the level of "phyical process" explanation because the "conceptual classification" issue has been resolved in the act of naming.

This sounds such an attractive proposition that one is tempted to jump in on the side of the debunkers, because surely one is saying that without the animistic ETH and similar tosh we could get on with some science. But this is not correct reasoning. The success of this strategy in the case of ball lightning does not guarantee that it will translate to the case of UFOs despite the centuries of momentum behind the success of naturalistic theories everywhere else in physics.

The fact is that today the notion of intelligent life elsewhere (in a quantum cosmos where "elsewhere" acquires an increasingly boggling spectrum of definitions) is a naturalistic concept with wide currency in physics. Like the crude principle of self-contained stable plasmas in the free atmosphere in 1930, it isn't yet a useful explanation of anything. But it could be. This is the door which somehow has to be held open against the pressure of what feels like irresistible improbability.

It is understandable – even, in some way, commendable – that an incompatible idea transplanted into the body of science risks triggering a sort of psychological tissue rejection. Modern minds are accustomed to classifying and systematising the world around them in a more focused way than "natural philosophers" were once wont to; the scientific trophy cabinet is packed to the doors, and there is little room today for the sort of vague tolerance that in centuries past might have been happy to call these events "tropospheric pseudo-meteors" and leave them be. Today we either understand phenomena (broadly speaking), or we are in the process of polishing up our understanding, or else we are clearing them out with all the uppish vigour of a house-proud hostess appalled by the discovery of a piece of cheap china behind the silverware.

Tropospheric pseudometeors? If such a classification had any sensible scientific meaning then we would no doubt chorus, "Ah yes, of course!" and it would no longer be necessary to whinge on about the fallibility of human perception, the absence of material evidence, of films and instrument readings, and people could simply get on with the job. The incident would suddenly be snatched from the fuscatory darkness into the light of Science, who would smoothly claim it for her own and build an academic discipline of Tropospheric Pseudometeoritics.

But then isn't this the point? There is no such discipline precisely because there is no proof that it would have anything to study, and there can be neither proof nor progress without hard data. How can there be a science of memories, probabilities, paper histories, hunches and inferences? Okay, maybe something did leave its mark momentarily on a few human retinas in 1956, and maybe its radar echoes did leave their glowing traces for a few seconds on the tube phosphor of a few radar scopes. But how can we do research without something to get our hands on, something that absolutely cannot be gainsaid? Maybe something was there, and maybe not; but even if it was, it has long gone and we don't know what it meant.

The Lesson of Ball Lightning for Ufology

And perhaps we never will. But by a serendipitous quirk of fate, on August 12 that year – about 9.00 am GMT on the very day before our UFO reportedly pursued a jet over Lakenheath – an instructive and analogous event occurred 1800 miles away in the skies over the lower Tambovsk region of what was then the USSR. A glowing reddish-orange sphere approached a commercial aircraft flying near thunderclouds at 10,000 feet. It was ahead of the aircraft off the port side and closing rapidly. Watched by three aircrew from the flight deck it passed close by the nose then suddenly swerved back around the fuselage and impacted the port propellor with a flash of light and an audible explosion that rocked the aircraft. Upon landing nothing, reportedly, was found except a very small fused area at the tip of one propellor blade and a small patch of soot that could be wiped off with a finger. Doubtless some sceptical meteorologists at the time explained that a smudge of soot was not really proof of anything, that it was probably caused by a minor lightning strike of the usual kind and that the witnesses had mistaken retinal afterimages of a lightning flash for a swerving ball of fire.

Now, I say all this happened. Possibly you even believe me. And why not? Today this story appears in scholarly discussions of ball lightning, generally cited without question not as something that happened "reportedly" but as a matter of historical record. "Cases like this are not unusual," remarked Altschuler complacently, telling this very story in the Condon Report without feeling the need even to reference it.[11] You maybe feel an urge to go and interview ageing witnesses or translate yellowing maintenance logs scribbled in Cyrillic pencil. But I doubt it. And yet is this mysterious aerial phenomenon really much different from the phenomena we are considering here? Is that ambiguous mark – which was (we are told) found on the tip of a long-scrapped Soviet propeller blade nearly six decades ago, and which no one reading this has ever touched or seen – so very much more real than the luminous marks which appeared on US and British radar screens a few hours later?

One's instinct is to reply: "Ah, but we could have touched and measured that mark ourselves, had we been there, and someone did. That it was not us is merely an historical accident." Indeed. And we could have observed and measured the radar blips at Lakenheath, Bentwaters and Neatishead, too, had we been there; we could have flown that RAF Venom jet, had we been there; maybe we could have seen that blur of light speeding over the Bentwaters airfield, and seen the erratic manoeuvres of other lights over Lakenheath, had we been there. A number of people were there, and they say they did.

But although there are certainly epistemological parallels to be drawn - and, it may be, physical ones too - between the Lakenheath/ Bentwaters sightings and ball lightning, in comparison with many of the extrovert traits of so-called ball lightning those UFOs seem relatively staid. None of them entered an aircraft cockpit to burn

off the pilot's eyebrows, for example, or inexplicably undid all the metal screws in a piece of telegraph apparatus, or spiralled around a domestic kitchen before carrying away several curing hams up the chimney and scattering them in the street – all of which have been earnestly reported by ball lightning witnesses. Instead we have to account for luminous bodies in generally linear (sometimes rectilinear) motion through the sky, one of which behaved as though drawn towards an intercepting aircraft. Why should this be so very preposterous? The luminous something that reportedly overflew Bentwaters did so at tremendous speed, but not faster than a charge might track along a conductor for instance. And the Lakenheath primary object behaved possibly in a capricious but not in a supernatural fashion. There is no reason to suppose that these behaviours could not be understood with a little effort, and it may be that the physics of ball lightning is a good point from which to start.

One tactical reason is that calling a phenomenon "ball lightning" simplifies an agonisingly raddled epistemology – it does wonders for witness credibility. When scientists cite dramatic tales of ball lightning they don't apply forensic chain-of-evidence rules with the same pedantic rigour that they are wont to insist on in the case of UFO reports. This is not because the eye-witness evidence they're citing is of a different character; it's because the existence of a consensus allows them to lighten up and start to think positively instead of curling up and thinking negatively of what they stand to lose.

John Rimmer, editor of the long-running Fortean magazine *Magonia*, suggests: "Misinterpretations, radical or otherwise, may well be as significant a part of ball lightning sightings as they are of UFO reports. However, as science has established a comfortable phenomenological niche for such reports, perhaps the impetus to identify and eliminate misinterpretations from the data base is not as strong amongst ball lightning researchers?"[12]

This is very possibly true, and it would be interesting to suggest to ball lightning physicists that they should study UFO research with a view to sharpening up their attitude to their data. What, I wonder, would they take from it? What would they make of the polarisation of psycho-social and physicalistic assumptions in this field? Would they be persuaded that the new physics they've begun to invent to explain ball lightning was unnecessary? Would they conclude that if only they'd known about ufology's RMP (Radical MisPerception) theory earlier then they needn't have bothered?

Probably not, because they and RMP are old friends. They've grown apart from it, and are embarrassed by that immature liaison. ball lightning physicists don't really like to be reminded of the fact that the first scientific explorers into ball lightning-land had a destructive effect on what had for centuries been a commonplace acceptance. For lack of a good theory consistent with the unfledged physics of the day, lightning balls ceased to exist. All reports of it were explained away by a Victorian equivalent of the RMP theory. If the present orthodoxy refers to this fact it tends to be in language that celebrates the success of scientific hard work, of which in fairness there has been a great deal. But I never hear an apology to the witnesses. I never hear an admission of any failing. Of course the blame lies at the door of a vanished – or vanishing – era and one cannot take responsibility for the past. Still, to me this loud silence does speak of a lesson not learned.

The lesson of ball lightning for ufology is twofold:

Firstly, one needs to be careful about drawing a general conclusion from the fact that a theory of misperception is plausible in general and demonstrable in particular cases. A catalogue of resolved cases is not a theory. As John Rimmer points out: "If ball lightning, like UFOs, only exists via eyewitness reports, it seems to me that the general scientific acceptance it has received, vis-a-vis UFO reports, is probably unjustified, and perhaps here is an area where some IFOs might be reclassified as UFOs with sufficient investigation."

This is probably quite true. There is nothing in science or logic that says signal cannot coexist with noise. In fact the situation in any sampling is that noise is universal, and a set of data which has too-sharp a peak of pure signal with no noise would typically suggest fraud, or a filter due to some artifact of the measurement process.

Secondly - and this is a lesson that has redoubled relevance for the internet generations – it is not enough just to assemble catalogues of mysteries. Mysteries do not constitute new knowledge. A list of unresolved anecdotes is not a theory either. The sceptics are right that they do not have to take a residue of intriguing mysteries seriously until someone comes up with a link-by-link chain of evidence matched to a testable new theory that predicts specific measurable effects.

But at the same time that doesn't mean that it is the sceptic's role to discourage such efforts – that is the debunker's role and it can be done without. It is useless to science. No testable theory was ever produced by negativity and pessimism.

On methodology in science Percy Bridgeman wrote: "The only possible attitude to the facts of experience as it unrolls is one of acceptance ... In particular, since there is no means by which we can foresee the future we cannot tell in advance whether any mental device or invention will be successful in meeting new situations, and the only possible way of finding out is to try it."

This is what happened with ball lightning. Cerillo in the 1940s and Kapitsa in the 1950s, then others, began to explore the "what if?" questions. They tried out the idea that at least some witnesses were describing something real and novel and came up with sketches of theories. Some of their peers then started to get the idea that maybe physics could model ball lightning after all, and that's how the stories changed from old-wives' tales to reports. All of a sudden, what had previously been hearsay of no probative value now became a fit subject for research grants. Serious analysis was begun on collections of ball lightning tales – the same tales, not new and instrumentally validated ones.

The world-famous "rain barrel observation" wasn't an experiment in a refereed journal but was the subject of a letter to a newspaper in 1936! I still get a shiver of delicious irony from recalling Altschuler's sober contemplation of the constraints placed on physical theory by the implied energy density of Mr. Morris's orange-sized lightning ball. No one at the Colorado University Plasma UFO conference seemed concerned that Mr. Morris may not have known a tangerine from a pomegranate or that his heirloom fob-watch might have stopped...

Then are the ball lightning theoreticians wrong? Is there no "new empirical phenomenon" called ball lightning? Or did they make a good judgement call on insufficient data and thereby generate a scientific conclusion whose value is becoming self-justifying? If they are right - and a virtual consensus now says that they are - this emphasises the importance of helping to facilitate a climate of productive and original theorising in anomalistics alongside a rigorous winnowing of the noisy evidence base.

The history of how ball lightning came to be rehabilitated from the outer darkness of mythology *can* of course fairly be described, with hindsight, as a success of science; but it ought not itself to be mythologised as a victory of the scientific hero over the dragon of popular superstition. Rather, it shows science happening as a social activity, the opportunistic product of a difficult but fruitful tension between cultural forces, in which cynical testing and naive openness to possibility (only rarely able to coexist in an individual) both have roles to play. Somehow it succeeds, almost despite us, in a pattern we are fated (I deliberately do not say "condemned") always to repeat because understanding is possible only in hindsight.

Martin Shough is a Research Associate for the National Aviation Reporting Center on Anomalous Phenomena (at the invitation of Dr Richard Haines, ex-NASA Human Factors head and NARCAP Chief Scientist) and is author or co-author of a number of papers and other publications. His main interest has been radar events. He has worked with several international collaborations to study cases in different parts of the world going back to 1946, and is the originator of a major ongoing effort to compile an historical catalogue of such events. He was trained in photographic and print science at London College of Printing (now London College of Communication, University of the Arts London) and was a landscape artist and gallery-owner in the Highlands of Scotland for many years. He has also been a semi-professional folk musician. His website is www.martinshough.com, and he can be reached via email via parcellular@btinternet.com.

THE
ANCIENT EGYPTIAN
DECAN ZODIAC

New research suggests ancient astronomy is a myth

by *Joanne Conman*

y research into ancient astrology has been ongoing for over 20 years. It's what led me to investigate the ancient Egyptian decans. Some thirteen years ago, I discovered a solution to the correct understanding of an ancient Egyptian text concerning the Egyptian zodiac. I published my findings in a scholarly journal of Egyptology. My solution to understanding the decan system works so well with the sky and is so simple, it never ceases to amaze me that no one else found it before I did. In the nearly eleven years since I first published, no one has demonstrated that my model is wrong; perhaps because it isn't. Instead, the academic establishment has reacted publicly to my work by refusing to engage. Scholars and scholarly groups have ignored or belittled my work (and me) as much as possible. Behind the scenes, there has been strong action to silence me. Why? Why not simply deal with my theory in good faith? It's testable, why not test it? If I am wrong, that would be the way to prove it. I have been forced to conclude that my theory is not wrong; rather, the powers that be have decided that I am the wrong person to have found it. But failing to deal with demonstrable truth does not help Egyptology or archaeoastronomy.

I have continued to dig deeper, to research further. I began to see a different and more consistent view of what the Egyptians were really doing with the stars and how it figured into their time-centered religion. I published two more academic papers and continued to find more and more intriguing material. Eventually, my research led me to the sources of Egyptology's most cherished dogma: the notion that ancient Egyptians practiced astronomy. The belief that ancient Egyptians practiced astronomy is perhaps the least critically researched, yet most unquestionably accepted conviction held about ancient Egyptians by academics. Astronomy is a modern Western science that grew out of a certain worldview; it is not a synonym for star-gazing or sky-watching. Astronomy is more limited, more focused, and more narrow than sky-watching. Ancient sky-watching – in Egypt and elsewhere – incorporated elements of modern astronomy at times, but it included much more: horizon-watching, bird-watching, and modern meteorology as well as a cultural understanding of the sky and universe that was specific to each society.

Ultimately, my exploration into the origins of Egyptology's entrenched belief in ancient astronomy led to the publication of my first book, *Ancient Egyptian Sky Lore: Rethinking the Conventional Wisdom* this past October. Its focus is a major error that occurred in the early nineteenth century, the time when Egyptology came into being. That error was the misidentification of ancient Egyptian religious/astrological art as an astronomical map. Early scholars often made unwarranted guesses about what they thought artifacts were. The misunderstanding of the well-known round zodiac ceiling from the Temple of Hathor at Dendera is one of the grand prizewinning errors of all time. Because the art was misunderstood, early scholars completely missed the Egyptians' identification and understanding of the five visible planets. That original error spawned numerous other errors that were defended instead of being challenged or reconsidered. The acceptance of the original error was partly the result of the state of scholarship and science in the nineteenth century. Its later perpetuation was and is the result of the unquestioning allegiance of academics to their predecessors.

Early scholars believed they were looking at a post-Renaissance astronomical map when they looked at the round zodiac ceiling from Dendera. They did not realize such a map was an anachronism

Dendera 'Round Zodiac'

in Ptolemaic Egypt. They knew nothing of the true history of astrology or astronomy. As they saw it, the figures in the center of that ceiling represented constellations or stars located in the northern circumpolar region. But the map is actually a prototype of an ancient astrologer's board; the figures in the center are honored powers, not circumpolar constellations. Now you may be wondering, what's the big deal? Well, it's a huge deal because it means that the translations of every single ancient Egyptian text that mentions either the Big Dipper or Orion are wrong. The figure that has been identified as the Big Dipper in the center of the Dendera round zodiac ceiling is actually identified in other written texts as the planet Saturn. The figure that has been identified as Orion on that ceiling is likewise identified as Jupiter. Many more images of the planets in Egyptian art have been badly misunderstood or missed altogether. There are a number of related texts that refer to the other planets, and they have all been mistranslated and misunderstood. Our picture of what the Egyptians were really watching in the sky and our understanding of their understanding is wrong. All wrong.

In my book, I provide a solution to understanding much of the misunderstood Egyptian material. A great deal of the ancient Egyptian art and a number of texts that have proven troublesome for scholars can easily be understood in light of my findings. What's more, everything fits very well into the understanding I found. There is an internal consistency in the logic that has always been missing from the conventional wisdom of Egyptology when it comes to the sky. Once the names of the five visible planets are correctly recognized, many things begin to make very good sense in a way they never have before. I also challenge an idea that is taken as a given by everyone: the idea is that astrology was brought to Egypt from Persia or Mesopotamia. Most people think astrology was invented in Mesopotamia. Too much evidence suggests it wasn't. A great deal in astrology reflects ancient Egyptian philosophy and religious thinking. Furthermore, there is no

Detail of Dendera round ceiling showing the planets (shaded figures) in their astrological exaltations. Moving clockwise from the lowest shaded figure: Jupiter is just ahead of (or in front of) Cancer (the crab); Mercury, just ahead of Virgo (the virgin); Saturn, just ahead of Libra (the scales); Mars directly above Capricorn (the goat-fish); and Venus just ahead of Pisces (two fish).

evidence of such ideas in Mesopotamia until quite late; what is found there could have easily been imported from Egypt. The mainstream scholars' view has it all backwards.

Why is there such hostility to the idea that astrology originated in ancient Egypt? Ancient Greek and Roman astrologers have all told us astrology has deep roots in Egypt. There is considerable evidence to support their claims. Yet, there is strong resistance to the idea from most scholars and from many modern astrologers. All have bought into a thoroughly unsubstantiated myth that astrology was brought to Egypt in the last few centuries before Christ. A good, close look reveals there was never anything factual behind that myth. Certain scholars simply decided that's how it was and those scholars have never been challenged on their presumption until now.

ASTRONOMY VS ASTROLOGY

It's probably wrong to refer to what any ancient people were doing with the stars as astronomy or astrology without qualifying exactly what is meant since both words are loaded with meanings for us modern people. As we generally define them, neither word necessarily applies to what ancient Egyptians (or any other ancient people) were actually doing. The fact that the Egyptians observed certain stars is *not* evidence of astronomy. Astronomy is a modern science, which is the product of a worldview that never existed in the minds of ancient Egyptians. Modern astronomy, like modern science in general, grew out of the Hellenistic world. Modern astronomy is a relatively young, culturally specific phenomena of Western European thinking. Defining astronomy correctly as the study of the positions and motion of celestial bodies and phenomena and then restricting what many ancient people actually did to what we would call astronomy limits our understanding of those people and their thinking. Loosely defining astronomy to be a system of knowledge or beliefs about celestial phenomena is essentially meaningless in terms of ancient Egypt, since it is just as applicable to what we can define as astrology or as astral religion. In fact, astronomy, astrology, and astral religions are quite different from one another. An important distinction can be made by considering the reason behind the celestial observation. In all cases, knowledge is being sought, but the question posed by the seeker determines the answer that will satisfy.

We speak of sunrise and sunset, but in fact, the sun does not rise or set; the earth orbits the sun and it turns as it does so. That turning of the earth causes the sun to come into view on one part of the globe and to go out of view on another part. Our words "sunrise" and "sunset" are based on an optical illusion. How are such illusions affected by the logic imposed by another language? How does another way of thinking influence the perception of the reality behind the illusion? Language influences perception. The languages of ancient people influenced their perception and helped to shape their unique and varied conceptions of cosmology. The explanations found in the cosmological model of one culture may not necessarily translate easily into the cosmological model of another culture. Based on what the texts tell us, the ancient Egyptians understood the sky – and the universe – quite differently from both the Greeks and the Mesopotamians, and therefore, quite differently from us. Our own views are inherited from the Greeks, with a heavy dose of Mesopotamian influence. Attempting to force Egyptian texts into the wrong model is part of what led to confusion and misunderstanding.

Modern astronomers seek the explanations of the workings they see in the heavens; the cause of the effect manifested. Their approach cannot be assumed to be the same as that of all or even some ancient star-gazers. Some ancient cosmologies were never intended as literal explanations of the physical universe, but were instead metaphorical.

Ancient religion is not pre-modern science as interpreted by ancient
people. Ancient astrology is neither proto-astronomy nor astronomy
fused with religious beliefs that are deemed unnecessary to modern
astronomers. Ancient astrology is also significantly different from
modern astrology. So it is inaccurate to refer to what ancient people
may have been doing with the stars as astrology, particularly with
modern astrology in mind. A number of different practices and
beliefs seem to have been synthesized into Hellenistic astrology,
which was itself a complex, ever evolving belief system.

Defining Astrology and its Apparent Roots

There are four branches of astrology in the West today that date
from ancient times. They did not all derive from the same source
originally. There has never been any good reason to think that
they did; although, as with the assumption of ancient astronomy,
the idea seems to be taken as given by everyone. First, we have
mundane astrology. Mundane astrologers analyze charts of
equinoxes, solstices, new moons, full moons, and other celestial
events to arrive at their forecasts, which are general predictions for
nations or sections of the world, for large groups of people, or for
the entire world. Mundane astrology is actually quite close to the
ancient Babylonian celestial omen-readings, which are what most
scholars and astrologers both accept as the ancestor of the whole
of Greco-Roman and later Western astrology. The Babylonian
astrologers looked at the same kinds of celestial happenings as
modern mundane astrologers: the equinoxes, solstices, lunations,
etc., as well as the positions of the planets in the zodiac. They
used them to make general predictions concerning world events;
for example, changes in the economy or wars between nations.
Mundane astrology is almost certainly a direct descendant of the
Babylonian omen readings.

Second, we have electional astrology. Electional astrology is used to choose the best time or at least avoid the worst time for any event or undertaking: a wedding, a trip, filing a lawsuit, buying a house, etc. This is what the Reagans used to select Ronald Reagan's inauguration times whenever they could. Electional astrology's appearance and use in the ancient world is attested in Greco-Roman times, but its origins are unclear. It appears to combine traditions from multiple sources.

Third, we have horary astrology which is true divination. An astrologer attempts to answer a question by casting a chart for the exact time at which the particular question was understood by the astrologer. Horary astrology has its own special set of rules which differ from those governing the other branches of astrology. Its charts are also interpreted differently from those of the other branches.

Many modern astrologers see electional astrology and horary astrology as two sides of the same coin. These two are actually quite different, which suggests that they came from different sources originally. Electional astrology focuses on planning a birth in some way, the birth of marriage, a business, whatever, and trying to control the forces that will influence that event so as to influence the entity or the undertaking itself. Horary is pure divination: it is throwing a question out there and seeing who answers as well as what the answer is. While both electional and horary probably incorporate ideas from several traditions, we see in Greek Egypt and Greco-Roman Egypt astrological divination that is much closer to later horary astrology than it is to any Babylonian omen-reading. Celestial divination is denied or wrongly attributed to foreign influences in Pharaonic times; however, it is there unquestionably and it is there quite early. Horary astrology has several elements in it that are consistent with earlier Egyptian thinking. A key example is the importance in horary astrology of the Ascendant. It hints at links to very ancient

Egyptian ideas because the Ascendant is the direct conversion of the ancient Egyptian eastern horizon, the *akhet*, into astrology. In Greco-Roman times, it was the spirit of the rising decan, that is, the deity of a certain section of the Egyptian zodiac, who came to answer the question. The decan spirits were invoked with lamps and they have survived in Middle Eastern folklore as the genie in the lamp.

The fourth branch of modern astrology is natal astrology, also known as genethlialogy. This branch of astrology deals with the influence of the planets and the signs on the life, destiny, and/ or character of an individual. Natal astrology is most clearly Egyptian in its origin. All over East Africa even today, the notion that something of the moment of birth remains with an individual throughout his or her life still exists. It is reflected in the naming practices. We also find this same idea in the Tetrabiblos of Claudius Ptolemy, who despite his Roman-Greek name, was an Egyptian who lived and wrote in Alexandria.

Ancient Egyptians believed that a person's fate was determined at birth; we have many examples of stories that show this. And those stories go way back; they are attested over 4,000 years ago. That means the Egyptian belief in fate being determined at birth was around centuries before there is any trace of our modern zodiac mentioned in Babylonian records and some 1,500 years before personal horoscopes are known in Mesopotamia. Like many modern East African names, ancient Egyptian names also reflect a link with the moment of birth through the names of the gods with whom the person had an affinity from birth. In Egypt, such beliefs date to the same time as the Egyptian decan zodiac. But that zodiac has not been understood by scholars and has not been properly studied. Its adoption into later astrology has been missed entirely because of the widely accepted wrong ideas about it that have become the dogma of Egyptology.

THE EGYPTIAN DECAN ZODIAC

At least 2000 years before ancient Greek astrology first appeared and several centuries before the Mesopotamians were writing about their constellations, the Egyptians had a functioning zodiac. The Egyptian zodiac consisted of thirty-six signs that worked with or as the Egyptians' calendar which consisted of thirty-six ten-day weeks, just like the modern twelve-sign zodiac works with our twelve-month calendar. Instead of one sign per month, the Egyptians had three signs per month; that is, one sign for each of their ten-day weeks. The name "decan" comes from the Greek word for "ten" from the ten-day weeks. The Egyptian decans were assimilated into the Greek zodiac as thirty-six 10° divisions of the ecliptic. Each decan survived into Greco-Roman astrology as one third of one of our zodiac signs. In later astrology, the decans are called faces or decanates in the West and *drekkana* in Vedic astrology.

Egyptologists have thoroughly misunderstood the ancient Egyptian zodiac because they have mindlessly followed the theory on its workings offered by the twentieth-century scholar Otto Neugebauer over a half century ago. Neither an Egyptologist nor an astronomer, Otto Neugebauer is still considered the ultimate authority on the so-called astronomical texts of ancient Egypt by most Egyptologists and archaeoastronomers. He was gifted in the study of languages, but had little feeling for anthropology. To see the ancients' world as they saw it did not seem to have interested him. He focused instead on the roots of modern western science, particularly the history of mathematical astronomy. That is a perfectly valid topic to research, but it is not anthropology nor is it theology. And it should never have been accepted as a substitute for either one when considering ancient Egyptian funerary art.

Neugebauer hypothesized that a non-existent belt of stars south of the ecliptic was the focus of Egyptian star-gazing and its stars were used to mark the Egyptian weeks. His model fails any way one tests it. Even with considerable contortions, no one has ever gotten it to work. Hypothesis testing is critical in science, so it is remarkably ironic that Neugebauer remains admired as a historian of science when he not only failed to test his own hypothesis, but also discouraged others from testing it. He never looked for a workable alternate hypothesis, which he would have had to do had he only tested his model. In contrast, my model works easily and is consistent with both the pattern of actual stars and the ancient Egyptian texts that describe how the decan system worked.

Approximately every ten days, the risings of particular stars on the eastern horizon marked the beginning of a new ten-day week for the Egyptians. We call the stars "decans" from the Greek word for "ten" and we sometimes call the Egyptian weeks "decades," meaning decades of days or ten days, the time of a decan. Generally, Egyptologists do not make any clear distinction between the spirit of the decan and the actual star that marked it. They should because these are separate and distinct concepts, as is the time period marked by the star. Four times in each year, a decan star was in one of four offices (or states or phases of existence). And in each ten-day Egyptian week, four stars occupied each of these offices, so that certain stars are grouped with other stars. Tables 1 and 2 (opposite page) show this; Table 1 lists the decans under their modern zodiac division as one third of our signs and Table 2 lists the decans by number in the Egyptian system. Both show the same pattern.

The ancient Egyptian decan zodiac functioned by recognizing each decan star to occupy four offices, states, or phases of existence over the course of a year. Each office was marked by the time of day that the star rose. The first of these offices or phases of existence is appropriately called "First." A decan star is First Star when it rises heliacally, which is rising just before the sun rises. Heliacal means "with the sun." The heliacal rise of the star Sirius marked the Egyptian New Year. Sirius set the pattern for all the decan stars and was considered to be their leader. Its deity, Sepdet, was a form of

TABLE I

FIRST	DUAT	BORN	WORK
ari 1	cap 1	lib 3	leo 1
ari 2	cap 2	sco 1	leo 2
ari 3	cap 3	sco 2	leo 3
tau 1	aqu 1	sco 3	vir 1
tau 2	aqu 2	sag 1	vir 2
tau 3	aqu 3	sag 2	vir 3
gem 1	pis 1	sag 3	lib 1
gem 2	pis 2	cap 1	lib 2
gem 3	pis 3	cap 2	lib 3
can 1	ari 1	cap 3	sco 1
can 2	ari 2	aqu 1	sco 2
can 3	ari 3	aqu 2	sco 3
leo 1	tau 1	aqu 3	sag 1
leo 2	tau 2	pis 1	sag 2
leo 3	tau 3	pis 2	sag 3
vir 1	gem 1	pis 3	cap 1
vir 2	gem 2	ari 1	cap 2
vir 3	gem 3	ari 2	cap 3
lib 1	can 1	ari 3	aqu 1
lib 2	can 2	tau 1	aqu 2
lib 3	can 3	tau 2	aqu 3
sco 1	leo 1	tau 3	pis 1
sco 2	leo 2	gem 1	pis 2
sco 3	leo 3	gem 2	pis 3
sag 1	vir 1	gem 3	ari 1
sag 2	vir 2	can 1	ari 2
sag 3	vir 3	can 2	ari 3
cap 1	lib 1	can 3	tau 1
cap 2	lib 2	leo 1	tau 2
cap 3	lib 3	leo 2	tau 3
aqu 1	sco 1	leo 3	gem 1
aqu 2	sco 2	vir 1	gem 2
aqu 3	sco 3	vir 2	gem 3
pis 1	sag 1	vir 3	can 1
pis 2	sag 2	lib 1	can 2
pis 3	sag 3	lib 2	can 3

TABLE II

FIRST	DUAT	BORN	WORK
28	19	12	4
29	20	13	5
30	21	14	6
31	22	15	7
32	23	16	8
33	24	17	9
34	25	18	10
35	26	19	11
36	27	20	12
1	28	21	13
2	29	22	14
3	30	23	15
4	31	24	16
5	32	25	17
6	33	26	18
7	34	27	19
8	35	28	20
9	36	29	21
10	1	30	22
11	2	31	23
12	3	32	24
13	4	33	25
14	5	34	26
15	6	35	27
16	7	36	28
17	8	1	29
18	9	2	30
19	10	3	31
20	11	4	32
21	12	5	33
22	13	6	34
23	14	7	35
24	15	8	36
25	16	9	1
26	17	10	2
27	18	11	3

the goddess Isis. The time a star is First lasts for one ten-day week. Ninety days after it is First, a star becomes the *Shen Duat* star for that ten-day week. *Shen Duat* has two meanings; it means Enclosed by Praises and it means Enclosed by the Light. The star rises late at night, marking the Dark Hour of Middle Night, a significant time in ancient Egyptian mysticism. The Dark Hour, the *ushau* hour, is the time each night when time resets itself and the gods Osiris and Re experience a mystical union that allows the universe to continue. The time a star was *Shen Duat* was when the star was in its most holy, most powerful, and also its most dangerous form. The *Shen Duat* star disappears at dawn in the middle of the sky, enclosed by the dawn's light. Seventy days after it is *Shen Duat*, the star is called Born. During that ten-day week, the star that is Born rises just after sunset. That is called the acronychal rise. When there is a full moon, the acronychal rising star rises with it. Eighty days after that, the star is said to Work or Serve. The Egyptian agricultural calendar had three four-month seasons. The working or service period was a decan star's personal season of one hundred twenty days. The Servant star appears somewhere in the middle of the sky after sunset, having risen hours earlier in the daylight. It is seen further and further in the western sky in the evenings until eventually, towards the end of the one hundred twenty-day period, it disappears altogether, becoming invisible because of its conjunction with the sun. Its next appearance is as First Star, when it once again rises ahead of the sun, just before sunrise.

In the two tables, you can see that certain decans are grouped with others. There is a relationship between the decans that occupy the four offices in each and every ten-day week. Knowing which stars were paired with which other stars in this system enabled the priests to know which week it was even if they could not see a morning or evening rise because of viewing conditions. Knowing which star was *Shen Duat* by its association with its mates allowed the priests to be certain when it was the Dark Hour. The priests knew in any given week which star should mark that hour because of its relationship with the morning and evening rising stars. Such knowledge is comparable to the way we know the relationships among the signs in our own zodiac; we know when the sun is in Capricorn, the constellation of Capricorn (though invisible) is rising at dawn while simultaneously, Cancer is setting and Aries is on the midheaven.

The Spiritual Side of the Decans

The earliest tables we have of the decans simply list their names. These lists were found on the coffins of over a dozen military leaders, dated over 4000 years ago. Individual decan spirits are mentioned by name in much earlier religious texts, but we have no record of them as an ordered group until these coffin star tables. Some 500 years later, lists of the decans appear in many royal tombs with their gods depicted beneath them. A few centuries later, we find lists of decans in both royal and non-royal tombs and on coffins with the decans taking on their own appearances. The portrayal of their images for the first time may be related to the rise of a cult that worshipped them. The decan spirits were portrayed as fantastic animals, composites of several creatures or as human figures with animal heads resembling typical ancient Egyptian gods.

The decans were not shown in the kind of consistent forms that the Greek and Babylonian zodiac signs were. The Greek zodiac signs derived from the Babylonian constellations which were linked to certain Mesopotamian gods. Those images did not change. The decan images are quite varied, probably because the decan spirits themselves had such changeable natures. It is possible that there were regional differences in the way the decans were portrayed. We possess lists of decans from different regions of Egypt which included alternate names for some decans.

The decans were feared as dangerous death dealers when they were in the *Shen Duat* phase, but the same spirits could be protective and nurturing when they were in another phase. And they could be male or female. In each of the four offices they held over the course of a year, the decan spirits had different powers. The same star spirits played different roles in their different states. Each office or phase of existence evoked different qualities from a star or its deity. The unique combination of the four in any given decade of days is what gave that time, that decan sign, its unique character. What controlled them was time itself. One of the chief contributions of the Egyptians to later astrology is the idea of variability based on time. Today, astrologers follow the Greek adaptation of that Egyptian idea. They see planets in different signs and houses as being stronger or weaker in influence and effect. A planet's location is totally controlled by time and any change in its nature is also controlled by time.

A cult that worshipped the decan spirits originated in southern Egypt nine centuries before Christ. It flourished for well over a thousand years before disappearing in about the sixth or seventh century AD. It spread as far as Carthage and Rome, as well as into parts of the ancient Near East and deeper into Africa, to Meroe. From all around the Mediterranean and North Africa, numerous amulets and amuletic jewelry have been found invoking the blessings of certain decans and providing needed protection from others. Many illnesses were believed to be caused by the spirits of the decan stars when they were in the dangerous *Shen Duat* phase. They were called Arrow demons in that office. Specific illnesses were linked with specific stars. Some amulets contain spells invoking protection from certain stars and seeking the protection of other stars. In Greco-Roman times, certain stones were associated with certain decans. Astrological amulets were made of carved cabochon stones or cameos that could be worn in jewelry or carried by a person. Many medical amulets have decanal connotations.

Despite the fact that it was apparently a wide-spread religion that lasted for many centuries and spread over a large area, scholars have devoted little time to the study of the decan cult. That's probably because they remain so confused about the decans and the Egyptians' view of the stars. In addition to surviving as genii, as mentioned above in connection with horary astrology, the decan spirits also survived as demons and angels in the *Testament of Solomon,* a work by a Greek-speaking Christian Jew or Jewish Christian that has been dated as early the first or second century AD, though it may be a little younger than that. Regardless, it deals with much older material. The story is meant to be a tale written by King Solomon himself concerning the building of his temple. The section dealing with the decan spirits involves a young boy who was working on the temple, who was a favorite of the king, and who was plagued by a demon. Solomon prayed to gain authority over that demon. He received a magic ring from God that was delivered to him by the archangel Michael. It was described as having a seal made of an engraved stone, very much like the Greco-Roman era astrological or decan amulets.

Sah (mistaken for Orion for over 200 years) and Sepdet, deities of the summer solstice. Sah is *not* Orion!

With his powerful ring, Solomon invoked thirty-six demons, who are the decans, and made each of them reveal their names, the stars to which they are connected, and how they can be controlled. Angels, some materials, and certain rituals or words have power over them. The *Testament of Solomon* is a particularly interesting text because the control the angels or good spirits have over the demons or dangerous spirits seems to follow exactly what we see in late native Egyptian astrology, which was especially focused on illnesses and dangers caused by the stars. Decans in one form have power over decans in another form, the power to overcome or control them. The *Testament of Solomon* hints that there is so much more to be understood about the spiritual side of the decans.

The early-mid fourth century AD astrological author Julius Firmicus Maternus' *Mathetheos Libri XVIII* is one of the few later texts that list the decan spirits by their Egyptian names, though the names he gives are quite garbled. Yet, Maternus' list is intriguing because it looks as if he may have had a copy of a specific intact decan list, one which is earliest attested nearly 1,700 years before his own time. The late fourth/early fifth century AD astrological author Hephaestio or Hephaestion of Thebes also possessed a list of decans, different from that of Maternus, but with some slightly less garbled names. Hephaestion incorporates two different lists of Egyptian decans. The major portion of his compilation follows one, but about one quarter of it includes material from a second, different list. This composite brings together decan lists from two different areas of Egypt that also appear to date from two different time periods, centuries apart. How these particular two came to be combined is unknown; how Hephaestion came by his list is also a mystery.

Decan lists derived from Hephaestion's and Maternus' lists made it to many places and survived into the late Middle Ages. A list made it to India and is incorporated in the work the Yavanajataka of Sphujidhvaja, a Sanskrit work on Greek nativities. Another list is also incorporated in Abraham Ibn Ezra's twelfth-century treatise *The Beginning of Wisdom*. Images and/or descriptions of the decans also appear in both the Yavanajataka and *The Beginning of Wisdom*, as well as in other later material such as the work of Cornelius Agrippa and in the work of the sixteenth century English physician and astrologer William Salmon. The spirits are only partially recognizable from earlier Egyptian portrayals, but there are some survivors that can be still be recognized.

Very little of the material related to the spiritual side of the decans has been studied. Whether one classifies it as astrology, partial astrology, or purely religious, this material deserves good scholarly research. The decidedly non-astronomical side of the decans is of no interest to astronomers and historians of astronomy who are typically uncomfortable with religious ideas and so, have little insight to offer. Because they have stuck with Neugebauer's erroneous decan theory, Egyptologists have misunderstood the decan system and how it truly worked. The direct assimilation of the decans into the Greek zodiac has been denied by Egyptologists and the astronomers who follow them. As a result, the decans' natures and powers that were incorporated into Hellenistic astrology have not been examined at all. Even worse, there are many academics who simply refuse to study astrology's history seriously. Those who do tend to focus on the astronomy they can find. Some astrologers have attempted serious study of the history of astrology, but they have done a poor job because they tend to use incomplete and outdated material. They offer little original research. And they tend to follow the mainstream academic view simply because it's the mainstream academic view. The powers that be have said that astrology did not exist in Egypt before the Greeks imported it. Astrologers have too happily bought into that myth, rather than to question or investigate.

Too many people have deferred to the mainstream academic view without realizing what is behind that view and what is missing from that view. The research that has been done based on Neugebauer's wrong decan model has led many scholars to draw wrong conclusions. They have missed the reality of the sky for the ancient Egyptians. Of greater concern is the enormous amount of research that has never been done at all concerning the planets because of a mindless devotion to a wrong idea perpetrated for more than two centuries by Egyptologists and astronomers. Because Jupiter was mistaken for the constellation Orion and Saturn was mistaken for the Big Dipper, everyone has missed and misunderstood what the Egyptians left behind. The importance of the planets to the Egyptians has been missed. Ancient Egyptian knowledge of the planets is considerable and very ancient. The oldest written records we have mentioning the names go back to the time of the Pyramid texts, some 4,500 years ago. All these records need to be re-examined now. The spiritual

Section of the Dendera linear zodiac, showing the decans Djat, Pehwey Djat, Tjemat, We-shaty, and Bekaty. They are pictured right to left under Virgo and Libra: Djat is under the two hour goddesses walking ahead of Virgo; Pehwey Djat is under the image of Virgo, the woman holding an ear of grain, as well as under the bull-headed figure and the image of Mercury in its day house, shown as an animal-headed bird; Tjemat is under the two hour goddesses preceding Libra; Weshaty is under the scales of Libra and the image of Horus in the solar disk; Bekaty is under the image of Venus in its day house of Libra.

side of the planets for the Egyptians remains completely unexplored. And there is a long history of what we might call pre- or proto-astrology in Egypt that has not been studied at all.

As long as Egyptologists are comfortable allowing Egyptology to exist as an exclusive private club, all will lose. New research should not be judged by the name on the byline but by the value of its substance. Ideally, scholars should approach new ideas with intelligence and curiosity, not with prejudice and a pathological fear of the unknown. I hope that my book will open some eyes and some minds, though after more than ten years, I'm not holding my breath. Regardless, I remain an inveterate researcher and my research will continue. It's just too fascinating to stop.

Joanne Conman is an independent scholar and anthropologist who has spent over twenty years researching ancient astrology, focusing on ancient Egypt and the stars for over fifteen years. Her research discovered a demonstrably correct understanding of the ancient Egyptian decan zodiac. She has published several papers in scholarly journals and has been a presenter at learned society conferences in Egyptology. Her first book, *Ancient Egyptian Sky Lore: Rethinking the Conventional Wisdom*, challenges Egyptology's most cherished dogma: the notion that ancient Egyptians practiced astronomy by revealing the correct identities of the five planets in Pharaonic Egypt, found in an ancient Egyptian textbook. You can find out more about Joanne's research at her website, www.joanneconman.com.

THE BOOK OF DEATH
...AND BEYOND

The Tibetan Book of the Dead and modern accounts of death:
A brief comparative analysis

by *Daniel Bourke*

The Tibetan book of the dead, as the work is commonly known, is an ancient text which was written for the purpose of helping the dying – and indeed, the dead – navigate the many geographies and challenges of the otherworld which comes after death; the *Beyond* as it has been called. It is a testament to the great attention paid by at least some of our ancestors to the dying process. Death after all, *is* a process, and one which is as natural and regulated as any other in the world.

Belief in the existence of an eternal soul is certainly one of the most common and longest held of all mans ideas. In today's increasingly non-religious, industrialized world, our notions of what births and constitutes a religion are extremely quaint and far removed from the visceral and deeply real psycho-physical experiences which lie at its core. Those ancient men whom stood apart from the institutions which would later build themselves around his experiences and claim to be the sole arbiter's of these mysteries, were the subjects to a truly affecting and shockingly personal experience. This was pointed out by transpersonal psychologist Holgar Kalweit when he wrote, "Ideas about the soul and about such states as the OBE (Out of body experience) are therefore not founded on abstract thought; their origin lies in genuine psychic experiences".[1] Modern religious institutions and their watered down doctrines are in practice, worlds apart from those genuine psychic experiences which underlie them. Those moving experiences which caused man to wonder in solitude at the vastness and beauty of the cosmos, and to shudder in humility at his own place in such a thing.

The idea here is simply to analyse the contents of the book of the dead, in its descriptions of the realm of death, with the relatively modern Near Death Experience (NDE) accounts and indeed induced contact with similar realms, in order to see if we can account for the key features of the former referencing the latter. In other words, can we look at the myriad set of "universal potential elements" reported of the NDE, in its more modern context, and find similar elements as have been reported in the book of the dead? Any resulting implications will be left up to the reader to decide for themselves.

The Near Death Experience

A number of authors in the field have repeatedly identified some key elements which occur during the greater majority of NDEs, themes which appear again and again; hence, while looking for parallels, we will lend greater credence to the search, by using primarily those

NDEs with such previously established consistencies intact. These include, but are not limited to, the Out of Body Experience, apparent contact with deceased relatives, contact with a being of light, a life review and the perception of a "barrier" or "point of no return" on the journey. There are many more commonalities between experiences and much more to be said in this regard, but that is far beyond the breadth of this particular work. A future piece will however deal with these in greater detail and it is enough to know that there are these established commonalities.

A Reflected World

There is not actually a huge amount of data to be drawn from the Book of the Dead, it is extremely succinct in its painting of the world beyond and in many ways it is a necessarily repetitive piece which is less a book in the traditional sense than it is an instruction manual. The text itself is predominantly concerned with those whom have found themselves on the other side of the veil and are either too overcome with terror or too wrapt in awe to take the steps necessary in order to proceed to the "summerland" beyond. Indeed akin to the experience of the inexperienced lucid dreamer who must similarly learn to hold both the fearful and the numinous aspects of his dreamtime at arm's length, instead practicing a sort of detachment. This means there aren't a massive amount of separate elements or phenomena in the text which describe the landscape of the Beyond and we will therefore be able to cover the majority of key features which its authors have said distinguish the Land of the Dead from our own in this comparative analysis.

Throughout the Tibetan text, many different guidelines are given in the hope that the dead will either be aware of them, by making himself aware of the teaching during the course of his earthly life or that he may be guided by its words by someone still in the land of the living so as to proceed without troubles. But there is one particular point that is made more than any other. The texts authors considered it the height of importance to inform its readers that the apparent limbo-like state which connects this life to the next is exquisitely and wholly responsive to the conscious and subconscious mind of the individual. And this was meant in quite a literal sense as the text explains…."Alas! When the Uncertain Experiencing of Reality is dawning upon me here, with every thought of fear or terror or awe for all [apparitional appearances] set aside, may I recognize whatever [visions] appear, as the reflections of mine own consciousness".[2]

This is a point made again and again throughout the text and it is representative of a broader theme which reveals itself to readers of the literature on the afterlife, and incidentally, many altered states in general, that metaphor and symbology are some of the key currencies of communication in these otherworldly realms. As the text goes on to say, "O nobly-born, all those are the radiances of thine own intellectual faculties come to shine. They have not come from any other place.[3] "The world beyond this one, according to descriptions, is uniquely susceptible to the thought processes of the individual and in many ways, at least initially, tailors itself to accommodate those environments and worldly appearances that he is used to. Indeed in many instances, those being who populate the beyond explicitly state that they are appearing in a way familiar to the traveller so as to comfort him during this time of great change and transition. This is a very important point in the general appreciation of the literature. One of the more well known modern accounts is in agreement here, that of George Richie who in the midst of an initially terrifying NDE wrote that "…whatever anyone thought, however fleetingly or unwillingly, was instantly apparent to all around him, more completely than words could have expressed it".[4]

Consider also the case of a Zuni tribesman whom, while visiting the world beyond this one himself, was told by an apparition that, "In order that this journey, which is long, might not seem strange to you, I have brought a couple of fine horses, such as my people used and I see your people use constantly nowadays".[5]

Philosopher A. J. Ayers reflecting on his own NDE had this to say. "Did you know that I was dead? The first time that I tried to cross the 'river' I was frustrated, but my second attempt succeeded. It was most extraordinary. My thoughts became persons".[6] Although it seems to be that Ayer did not have a wholly conventional NDE, his words reflect the role of thought not just in the post-mortal realm, but in states of mind which can be attained by a variety of other and related means.

Dr. Raymond Moody in his work, *Life After Life*, widely credited with revitalising interest in the topic of post-mortal survival, writes, "Interestingly, while the above description of the being of light is utterly invariable, the identification of the being varies from individual to individual and seems to be largely a function of the religious background, training, or beliefs of the person involved".[7] With this particular point made however, it is very important to note that although this is manifestly the case, it is only to a certain extent and within a particular context and that for the most part, the NDE is unexpectedly surprising to the dying person. It is generally out of step with what his religions or ideas have told him about the otherworld and it is deeply novel to him in many more ways than it is familiar. It is this novelty which sets these realms apart and which becomes even more intriguing when we consider the mysterious extent to which they are experienced consistently both across cultures and across time. It is enough to know that a defining feature of the NDE is both it's elements of familiarity, and their conflation with elements of striking unfamiliarity.

Heightened Mental Faculties

One of the more puzzling and persistent elements which has emerged from modern NDE accounts and is brought out again and again by many authors is the subjective experience of an enhanced intellect. Clear and lucid thought reported to be far in excess of what was possible before, and not just thought, but sight and hearing are also greatly enhanced. Even the hard of hearing and those with visual problems have reported these enhanced capabilities. And all this, in the majority of cases during a time of clinical death, flat brain waves and in some cases, deep coma. (Note: The definition of death itself is a rather contentious one. However without going into much detail on these definitions, it is enough to say, that in the case of the NDE, the most important thing in this absence of this information is not whether the person is dead as such, but rather how functional are his brain capacities, particularly those which afford or mediate cognition, during the time of the NDE and the recurring themes in the accounts of those either dead or near death, and indeed whether or not some aspect of the mind is mysteriously projected outward at this stage. It is less important whether or not the individuals biological processes have ceased, than it is important as to whether or not some aspect of the individual has left the body at this stage, this way we can leave the squabbling regarding the exact moment of death up to others)

The Tibetan Book of the Dead makes a similar claim. While speaking about how and why it is advantageous to read the book even once, the authors go on to state matter-of-factly that, "Through having heard it once, even though one do not comprehend it, it will be remembered in the Intermediate State without a word being omitted, for the intellect becometh ninefold more lucid [there]".[8] In a fascinating parallel, Raymond Moody whom has interviewed dozens of people who have had NDE's, writes that, "Over and over, I have been told that once they became accustomed to their new situation, people undergoing this experience began to think more lucidly and

rapidly than in physical existence".[9] To be more specific, a case from the study of Melvin Morse speaks of this phenomenon. "While he watched what was going on below him, he suddenly felt as though there had been a great increase in his intelligence".[10]

From Jeffrey Long's deeply extensive NDERF (Near Death Experience Research Foundation) study we find a case in which a woman had an NDE just after the birth of her 10th child, and after experiencing many of the classical elements of the NDE, went on to report that, "I felt myself to be very awake and aware the whole time, I was immensely curious and observing, and my awareness was unearthly, much larger than we I am here in life. I could see 360 degrees around myself; I could focus on what I wanted to and it close-up without any problems, even without thinking about it. I could look up, down, forward and behind me all at once".[11]

The experiences of Robyn from the NDERF study are also in line with this when she speaks of her clarity of awareness during her own NDE. She goes on to say that she had "more consciousness and alertness than normal.[12]

One of the more noteworthy accounts in its extensive detail is also in agreement on this point. Howard Storm was, for what it's worth

to the reader, something of a militant atheist by his own admission. He stated of his fascinating experience. "Obviously the first thing I thought about was, *Is this a hallucination?* Yet by every sensation of myself I knew that it wasn't a dream or a hallucination. It was actually more vividly real than normal consciousness.[13]

In 1795, Rear-Admiral Sir Francis Beaufort, narrowly escaping death reported that "though the senses were...deadened, not so the mind; its activity seemed to be invigorated, in a ration which defies all description, for thought rose above thought with a rapidity of succession that is not only indescribable, but probably inconceivable by anyone who has not himself been in a similar situation".[14]

Likewise, neurosurgeon Dr. Eben Alexander reporting on his own NDE, expresses surprise at the clarity of his thinking. "The more I learned of my condition, and the more I sought, using the current scientific literature, to explain what had happened, the more I came up by spectacularly short. Everything-the uncanny clarity of my vision, *the clearness of my thoughts*, a pure conceptual flow-suggested higher, not lower, brain functioning.[15]

In another case, we read that, "The mountains appeared to be about fifteen miles away, yet I could see individual flowers growing on their slopes. I estimated my vision to be about one hundred times better than on earth. To the left was a shimmering lake containing a different kind of water – clear, golden, radiant, and alluring. It seemed to be alive. The whole landscape was carpeted with grass so vivid, clear, and green, that it defies description".[16]

In yet another case related to Dr Jeffrey Long the NDE experient writes that," [I was] unconscious physically, but more alert/conscious than I had ever experienced before or since. Like a window had been cleaned that you did not know was dirty until you saw the difference.[17]

To clarify again, there is no attempt here to objectively prove that such states are conducive to higher awareness, but simply to find in the modern literature, analogous contents to those found within the Tibetan book of the dead, and according to those accounts, many more of which the reader will find within the works referenced here, are in agreement that as Arthur Yansen stated, the grass is quite literally greener on the other side.

Sight and Hearing in Those Lacking Both

One particularly interesting parallel lies in the texts sole statement to individuals who have had trouble with both sight and hearing in their earthly lives, and how they will find these impairments do not follow them into the Beyond. As the Book of the Dead states. "Thou mayst have been, when living, blind of the eye, or deaf, or lame, yet on this After-Death Plane thine eyes will see forms, and thine ears will hear sounds, and all other sense-organs of thine will be unimpaired and very keen and complete".[18]

Dealing with the experience of Bolette from the NDERF study, we find in her detailed account, her telling us that..." I have hearing loss in my life, I did not have that in death, and I could hear much better than ever in my life. I had no trouble with my hearing; the sounds were beautiful and melodic".[19]

One of the most famous NDE accounts is that of Vicki Umipeg who was born blind after an excess of oxygen in her incubator completely destroyed her optic nerve. The case is again, clearly of the classical variety with its well rounded roster of persistent elements. With the words of the Book of the Dead in mind, we will now look at Vicki's attempt to communicate her experience beyond the veil of life and death. "I had a hard time relating to it (i.e., seeing). I had a real difficult time relating to it because I've never experienced it. And it was something very foreign to me ... Let's see, how can I put it into words? It was like hearing words and not being able to understand them, but knowing that they were words. And before you'd never heard anything. But it was something new, something you'd not been able to previously attach any meaning to".[20]

In a case documented by Dr. Kenneth Ring in his 1984 book *Heading Towards Omega*, the NDE of a short-sighted woman is relayed as follows.."It was so vivid...they were hooking me up to a machine that was behind my head. And my first thought was, "Jesus I can see! I can't believe it, I can see!" I could read the numbers on the machine behind my head and I WAS SO THRILLED".[21]

In the case of Brian, which is also completely in line with the classical cases in that it shares a great many recognizable features which clearly demonstrate it as a genuine NDE, we find that although the man was born deaf, he had no problem speaking and being spoken to, albeit in a manner which he describes as "telepathic" during his time beyond life. "I was born profoundly DEAF and had all hearing family members, which all of them knew sign language! I could read or communicate with about 20 ancestors of mine and others through telepathic methods. It overwhelmed me. I could not believe how many people I could telepathize with simultaneously".[22]

Respected Cardiologist Dr. Pim Van Lommel who, along with his colleagues carried out an extensive ten year study which was published in the renowned medical journal *The Lancet* and the results of which are published in his seminal work *Consciousness Beyond Life,* had many more NDE's to offer and many of those again, tie into the assertions made in the Book of the Dead that those with afflictions of both hearing and sight will find themselves unimpaired in the post-mortal realm. As one of his informants goes on to say. "I saw the most dazzling colours, which was all the more surprising because I'm colour blind. I can distinguish the primary colours, but pastels all look the same to me. But suddenly I could see them, all kinds of different shades. Don't ask me to name them because I lack the necessary experience for that".[23]

Dr. Kenneth Ring and Sharon Cooper have compiled a great many more of these cases for anyone interested in further researches entitled *Mindsight,* and also of interest may be Chapter 7 in Chris

Carter's *Science and the Near Death Experience*. Anyone who wishes to read a more compacted thesis in this regard should refer to their excellent paper "Near-Death and Out of Body Experiences in the Blind: A study of Apparent Eyeless Vision", which addresses the issues of the NDE in blind individuals with great clarity.

TRAVEL AT THE SPEED OF THOUGHT

The text states unequivocally that while one is in the "Bardo-state", he has the ability to arrive at any destination he desires, merely by directing his mind to that destination. "O nobly-born, thou art actually endowed with the power of miraculous action, which is not, however, the fruit of any samādhi, but a power come to thee naturally; and, therefore, it is of the nature of karmic power. Thou art able in a moment to traverse the four continents round about Mt. Meru. Or thou canst instantaneously arrive in whatever place thou wishest; thou hast the power of reaching there within the time which a man taketh to bend or to stretch forth his hand".[24]

This has been a staple of the OBE nad NDE literature since the beginnig. Modern accounts are in full agreement and abound with exactly the same descriptions. Consider the case of an American informant named Lisa who, stumped at what to do next having found herself floating out of her body on the ceiling discovered that (according to her interviewers Barbara Walker, Dr. William Serdahely and Lori Bechtel), "the answer came to her immediately. She realized that all she needed to do was to let her mind tell her soul body where to move, and in doing so her soul would travel to that destination".[25] Her words mirror closely the description given in the book of the Book of the Dead.

In another case reported by Cardiologist Dr Michael Sabom, his informant states that, "I could see anywhere I wanted to. I could see out in the parking lot, but I was still in the corridor...It was just like

I said, *Okay, what's going on out in the parking lot?* And part of my brain would go over and take a look at what's going on over there".[26]

Indeed, American psychologist Charles Tart, testing the Out-of-Body or OBE phenomenon which is an essential element in the archetypical NDE under lab conditions, discovered and listed the most prominent and persistent elements, one of those being, "Suddenly being at a place of which you have just thought".[27] which again, is the same feature of the OBE state given in the Book of the Dead. One of his subjects went on to state that, "Back into the physical [body] was achieved simply, by [the] thought of return".[28]

INCAPACITY TO COMMUNICATE WITH THE LIVING

The Book of the Dead tells us early on that, "When the consciousness-principle getteth outside [the body, it sayeth to itself], 'Am I dead, or am I not dead?' It cannot determine. It seeth its relatives and connexionsas it had been used to seeing them before... and, although he can see them and can hear them calling upon him, they cannot hear him calling upon them, so he goeth away displeased".[29] The kind of frequency with which this is reported in modern and indeed ancient accounts is certainly food for thought. For the interest of the reader, this is particularly interesting in light of the notions that the NDE is somehow an "evolutionary comfort mechanism" for the dying, for what comfort is there in the dying man or woman being unable to communicate with the ones he holds the dearest? But moving on from this point which will be addressed in greater detail down the line, we can examine a few of those cases which are, as with all the cases presented in this piece, representative of a much greater number of documented cases which can be found in the publications mentioned and many other places besides.

In one account we read, "I saw them resuscitating me. It was really strange. I wasn't very high; it was almost like I was on a pedestal, but not above them to any great extent, just maybe looking over them. I tried talking to them but nobody could hear me, nobody would listen to me".[30]

In another, "People were walking up from all directions to get to the wreck. I could see them, and I was in the middle of a very narrow walkway. Anyway, as they came by they wouldn't seem to notice me. They would just keep walking with their eyes straight ahead".[31]

Another case still goes on to state "As I turned, my elbow came into contact with the arm of one of two gentlemen who were standing in the door. To my surprise his arm passed right through mine without apparent resistance, the severed parts closing again and again without pain, as air reunites. I looked quickly up at his face to see whether he had noticed the contact but he gave me no sigh".[32]

Sabom reports on the case of a construction worker who was injured, "One time a nurse I could see looked me right in the face just this far away [indicating one foot]. I tried to say something, but she didn't say nothing...She was like looking at a movie screen that can't talk back and that doesn't recognize you're there".[33]

While on of Raymond Moody's informants told him that, "It was really strange. I wasn't very high; it was almost like I was on a pedestal, but no above them to any great extent, just maybe looking over them. I tried talking to them but nobody could hear me, nobody would listen to me".[34]

Dr. Cherie Sutherland reports on a case of an Australian, who suffered a series of heart attacks as a teenager in school. "I was out of the body, and I thought to myself, *I must be dead*. So I went up to Miss Smith and told her not to bother, I was dead. She took no notice of me. I made a few more attempts to speak to her and to Miss Breen then gave up...".[35]

Meanwhile, Howard Storm reported, upon leaving his own body that he opened his eyes "and I was standing looking at my body in the bed, and I was standing right next to the bed. And there was my wife, and I started yelling and screaming at her, like, *Whats going on?*

How can I be standing up, looking at myself? And I felt completely real, and she didn't respond to me. And I gestured wildly, and I started swearing and screaming, and no response...I figured that she was crazy or something, so I turned around to my room-mate and started yelling at him. And the same thing, he was just like frozen".[36]

In closing this section, it may be of interest to some to note that I personally am yet to come across a case where this attempted physical contact between the dying and the living *has* been possible. And yet, the dying person can, in every case, speak with and respond to those beings he perceives as either dead or divine. The potential implications of this will be described in a later piece.

THE LIFE REVIEW AND THE MIRROR OF KARMA

The idea of a final judgment, of the weighing up of man's good deeds against his bad as a means of attaining what the Tibetans have called "Buddhahood" is as old as religion itself. The Life Review is a well documented if not statistically universal element of the NDE. It may not be as widely reported as for instance the Out of Body Experience; however it is reported widely enough to be considered one of the most intriguingly consistent elements across accounts. And each are coupled with some fascinatingly specific ancillary features such as the seeming capacity of the viewer to feel the emotions of those involved in the visions, and the literal tracing of the effects of one's actions through time and their actual effects on other people. The book of the dead is fairly short spoken on this matter however what is said is interesting enough to warrant some tentative comparisons.

Here is what the text's authors spoke of regarding the *Mirror of Karma*..."If thou neither prayest nor knowest how to meditate upon the Great Symbol nor upon any tutelary deity, the Good Genius, who was born simultaneously with thee, will come now and count out thy good deeds [with] white pebbles, and the Evil Genius, who was born simultaneously with thee, will come and count out thy evil deeds [with] black pebbles. Thereupon, thou wilt be greatly frightened, awed, and terrified, and wilt tremble; and thou wilt attempt to tell lies, saying, 'I have not committed any evil deed'. Then the Lord of Death will say, ' I will consult the Mirror of Karma'. So saying, he will look in the Mirror, wherein every good and evil act is vividly reflected. Lying will be of no avail".[37] The Tibetan Mirror of Karma then represents the experience of revisiting one's earthly life in detail.

The main difference between this and modern accounts (although even that is a stretch as no two modern accounts are exactly the same) is that there is a sense in these words, that the Lord of Death is himself personally judging the individual in her or her lifestyle and choices. Whereas the modern accounts for the most part, but not unanimously, describe that the individual is his own judge and jury. Comments such as *I reviewed my life, and I did the judging* are very common. This is not to speak on or imply that there is or isn't some universal moral code whereby any actions can be considered virtuous if the individual sees no wrong. It is just to say that the individual seems to be somehow aware of whether or not he has acted, within his capacity to do so, as agreeably as possible particularly in his behaviour and actions toward other human beings. At times this seems to be with reference to an outside value system, at times to their own, but these two things are not necessarily mutually exclusive. However the individual rarely feels a sense of condemnation from an outside source. If he feels any condemnation it is generally his own remorse, guilt and regret having watched himself act in a way he may not be proud of. And even in those accounts where perhaps there is a sense of outer condemnation or guilt, it is possible, based on what we have learned so far, that this too is some manner of projection of the individuals own feelings into the space around him.

Of course, this is just speculation. It is frequently stressed in many modern accounts that indeed, lying will be of no avail. Now, if we consider that the Book of the Dead is unequivocal on the fact that even the religious figures come forth from one's own mind, we can perhaps see the Lord of Death not as some final arbiter that each individual will meet, but rather a manifestation of the individuals own capacity to judge themselves.

An NDE experient named Samantha had a particularly detailed experience to share." At that point, I was totally unconcerned with whether I was alive or not. My focus was on what was being shown to me—a sort of film reel that was directly in front of me but up just a bit. It was like watching an immense, very clear TV. I was watching images of every event that had taken place in my life—my entire life all in pictures. The most interesting part of it was that with each picture—with all the pictures (there were more than I could count) I re-experienced the original feelings that had accompanied each one at the time it had actually happened".[38]

Our friend Howard Storm during his own NDE, before reporting on a life review had a dialogue with some beings which

he perceived. He asked them a question as follows, "Everything I think of, you respond to. Do you know what goes on in my mind?" And they replied, "Yes". Howard went on to ask. "What if I had a thought that I don't want you to know about?" To which the beings replied, "We know everything that you think about and we have always known everything that you have thought about." This is very much reminiscent of the line in reference to the mirror of Karma which states that *lying can be of no avail* and speaks more broadly on the seemingly transparent nature of thought in the Beyond. Storm then went on to detail his own life review. "My life played out before me, maybe six or eight feet in front of me, from beginning to end…Some things they slowed down on, and zoomed in on, and other things they went right through. They showed me my life in a way that I had never thought of before. All the things that I had worked to achieve, the recognition that I had worked for, in elementary school, in high school, in college, and in my career, they meant nothing in this setting…they didn't say that something was bad or good, but I could feel it. And I could sense all those things they were indifferent to…what they responded to was how I had interacted with other people".[39] Again we see the theme of the individual as the judge. It is interesting to note a less obvious parallel with the book of the dead here too. The beings Storm interacts with specifically tell him that they can appear to him in a way which might make him more comfortable, and we understand that this place is malleable by thought.[40] With this said, the Tibetan Lord of the Dead is again, likely just one manifestation of this one person's projection, indeed it may be based on the experience of just one *particular* person, although this is probably less likely.

From one of Dr. Raymond Moody's many informants we read that "Then it seemed there was a display all around me, and everything in my life just went by for review, you might say. I was really very, very ashamed of a lot of the things that I experienced because it seemed that I had a different knowledge, that the being of Light was showing me what was wrong, what I did wrong...it showed me not only what I had done but even how what I had done had affected other people".[41]

In the case of Swedish Anaesthetist Dr Goren Grip, we read that "I re-experienced everything that happened in my life and watched it as a spectator with the being. Most of what saw about me and my brother, of whom I was very jealous. My attention was focused on our exchanges of emotions, my jealousy, my feelings of triumph when I hit him, his surprise when I hit him for no reason his anger and resentment, and later his triumph when he got back at me... When I did something loving to him, I experienced my love, my brother's surprise, as well as his love and happiness. I experienced his feelings as clearly as my own, making this a fantastic lesson on the consequences of my own actions".[42]

Conclusions

The Tibetan book of the dead as it is casually known in the West, according to this analysis shares many correspondences with relatively modern accounts of the world as it has apparently been experienced beyond death. In fact, all of the key points which describe the nature of the world beyond our own are in complete agreement with modern accounts both generally and specifically.

The text speaks only of the transitory state between states, and is not attempting to chart the entire geography of the world beyond. There are many other traditions which claim to speak of the world beyond our own, not the least of which is the Egyptian book of the Dead. Although the details of these traditions are beyond the bounds of this piece, it is interesting to note, and perhaps something for the reader to follow up on, that the reason the title "Tibetan Book of the Dead" was chosen in the first place was due to the parallels that Dr. Walter Y. Evans-Wentz found between the text and the Egyptian book of the dead.

A relatively limited number of accounts have been presented here in the interest of both readability and succinctness. However if anyone is unsure as to whether or not they are representative of the broader canon of NDE accounts, they are invited to read the works of the authors mentioned through the course of this piece and they will be in no doubt as this fact. Although there are a select few similarities which are more often spoken about than others, there are many many more which are again both general and specific in detail which come from sources as far removed from each other as could be both culturally and across time. In the end, it is the persistent and mysterious universality of the Near-Death Experience which has from the beginning, been its defining feature, its greatest source of fascination and that which calls us again and again to probe ever deeper into the confounding nature of life, death and consciousness itself.

> "Cause it to come that there be neither awe nor terror in the Bardo"
>
> – *The Tibetan Book of the Dead*

Daniel Bourke is an independent author, artist and musician. He is currently in the process of writing *Further Explorations of the Near-Death Experience*, a book which he hopes will contribute meaningfully to the field of Near-Death Studies. Some of his other work can be read at http://tinyurl.com/m5wfnsd. Daniel can be contacted at daniel_bourke89@hotmail.com

BELIEVING IN *Fiction*

THE RISE OF HYPER-REAL RELIGION

"What is real? How do you define real?"
– Morpheus, in *The Matrix*

"Television is reality, and reality is less than television."
- Dr. Brian O'Blivion, in *Videodrome*

by *Ian 'Cat' Vincent*

Ever since the advent of modern mass communication and the resulting wide dissemination of popular culture, the nature and practice of religious belief has undergone a considerable shift. Especially over the last fifty years, there has been an increasing tendency for pop culture to directly figure into the manifestation of belief: the older religious faiths have either had to partly embrace, or strenuously oppose, the deepening influence of books, comics, cinema, television and pop music. And, beyond this, new religious beliefs have arisen that happily partake of these media

– even to the point of entire belief systems arising that make no claim to any historical origin.

There are new gods in the world – and and they are being born from pure fiction.

This is something that – as a lifelong fanboy of the science fiction, fantasy and horror genres and an exponent of a often pop-culture-derived occultism for nearly as long – is no shock to me. What did surprise me, however, was discovering that there is a growing area of sociological study of these beliefs… an academic realm which not only seeks to understand these developments, but also provides a useful perspective on modern belief for both the Fortean and the occult practitioner.

I first learned about this area of study from a 2007 interview on the excellent religion and pop culture focussed website *Theofantastique* with the Australian sociologist Dr. Adam Possamai,[1] in which he talks about his research into what he has termed 'hyper-real religion'.[2] Fascinated, I acquired his introductory text to the concept, *Religion And Popular Culture: A Hyper-Real Testament*[3] and, later, the mammoth 2012 collection of research and essays on the subject which he edited, *Handbook of Hyper-Real Religions*.[4]

The term 'hyper-real' itself draws on the work of the French postmodern theorist Jean Baudrillard. Possamai's current definition of hyper-real religion is;

> …a simulacrum of a religion created out of, or in symbiosis with, commodified popular culture which provides inspiration at a metaphorical level and/or is a source of beliefs for everyday life.[5]

Let's unpick that…

A key aspect of postmodern theory (especially poststructuralism, in which Baudrillard was a key writer) is that, in modern society, symbols have attained such importance that they have actually overtaken the things which they are symbols *for*. Baudrillard emphasises this particularly in his essay *Simulacra and Simulation*.[6] Here, he draws a distinction between *Simulation* – copies of an imitation or symbol of something which actually exists – and *Simulacra* – copies of something that either no longer has a physical-world equivalent, or never existed in the first place. His view was that modern society is increasingly emphasising, or even completely replacing, the simulation with the simulacra, the actual being displaced by the never-real... and that:

> ... The simulacrum is never that which conceals the truth – it is the truth which conceals that there is none. The simulacrum is true.

The term 'hyper-real' derives from this perspective: he defines it as "the generation by models of a *real* without origin or reality" (emphasis mine). The novelist and philosopher Umberto Eco later put this more succinctly, saying the hyper-real is "the authentic fake".[7] Although Baudrillard did not specifically discuss religion in this context, Possamai's use of the term fits broadly into Baudrillard's view that modern society is especially, if you forgive my pun, symbol-minded.

The other key word in the definition given by Possamai above is "commodified". It is a key aspect of postmodern and poststructuralist thought (which, though it stems almost entirely from the Marxist leanings of its founders, still has a remarkably apt bearing on our current situation) that the main cultural aspect of modern society is its origin in a time period which has almost completely succumbed to the viewpoint of neo-liberal concepts around value and trade – an era usually referred to as 'Late Capitalism', dating from roughly the end of WWII.[8] The late capitalist era is defined by the power of multi-national corporations, globalised markets and labour, increased concentration of financial speculation and (most significantly here) mass consumption. In the late capitalist world, pretty much everything can be defined or co-opted as a commodity, as Product.[9]

That's the thing about pop culture (and, of course, all cultures
– a factor Possamai does not neglect): it's bought and sold. And
it's this easily available aspect of it, in combination with the
Western World's emphasis on individuality and choice (thoroughly
reinforced by neo-liberal capitalist practices), which allows hyper-
real religion to bloom.

The one aspect of postmodern thought that has thoroughly
leaked into the overall modern mindset is the undermining of the
Grand Narrative concept, the long-standing belief that there is One
True Truth which underlies all aspects of a given society. While this
has possibly led to the 'clash of civilisations' strife that dominates
much of the geopolitical landscape,[10] it has also given the scope
for individuals to seek their own defining narratives and faiths. As
Possamai puts it:

> ...in this consuming world, the individual becomes his or her own
> authority; the postmodern person in the West no longer tolerates
> being told what to believe and what to do... he or she is faced with
> a proliferation of 'spiritual/religious/philosophical knowledges',
> which he or she researches and experiences.[11]

This personal seeking for truth has manifested in a variety of ways.
For some, it allows them to find new and vivid metaphors for their
existing beliefs. For others, it can give them the chance to move
beyond the beliefs of their kin and tribe to find other beliefs (or, of
course, to reject belief as a concept entirely). And, most interestingly
for me, it can bring some people to find or even create a whole new
range of faiths, based on the stories they find within pop culture.

If there is one thing we can say with certainty about the human
mind, it is that it has a core-deep hunger for narrative. It is in stories
that we have always found and transmitted our truths, probably from
as far back as we have actually had language. It is clear that, on some
levels, our minds react nearly identically to a story as to that which

the story is *about*. Whether or not the story happens to be, for want of a better word, 'true', doesn't matter for the most part.[12]

And these days, there are so very many stories to choose from.

Bearing all this in mind, let's look at some examples of hyper-real religion... and, especially, the particularly influential role played by the science fiction and fantasy genres.

HISTORY

"If you believe it's sacred, it's sacred."
- Irving Rosenfeld, in *American Hustle*

Finding a starting point for the rise of the hyper-real religions might seem a problematic thing. After all, the telling and retelling of tales where the true origin is lost to antiquity and thus subject to untold levels of embellishment and fantasising has been a problem in the consideration of the history of all beliefs. There is a fine line between the growth of a mythology and its outright invention – not least because all of the hyper-real beliefs have necessarily drawn on older mythologies for their mystical and philosophical approaches (for example, the Buddhist and Taoist roots of the Jedi in *Star Wars*, who I will return to in some depth later on).

There is also the particular case of the belief systems spawned by L. Ron Hubbard – Dianetics and especially Scientology were certainly a product of his prolific work in pulp fiction writing, as well as his liberal borrowing from the work of Aleister Crowley, which he encountered as a result of his friendship with (and/or infiltration of the branch of the Ordo Templi Orientis led by) Jack Parsons in 1940s California.[13] However, they cannot be shown to have derived from any particular fictional work.

We can, however, establish a firm date for the first religion to be based primarily on a fictional source – one which Possamai himself cites in *A Hyper-Real Testament*. The date was 7 April 1962, and the religion is The Church Of All Worlds.

Founded by the American Neo-Pagan priest Oberon Zell-Ravenheart and his friends, the name and initial ritual structure of The Church Of All Worlds (CAW hereafter) derives from the practices described in Robert A. Heinlein's novel *Stranger In A Strange Land* as  having been brought to Earth by the adopted Martian hero, Valentine Michael Smith – specifically the ninefold structure of the Church and a bonding ritual for members based on the sharing of water.[14] The CAW also drew heavily on Zell's Earth-based pagan spirituality and, later, other science fiction concepts such as the Vulcan philosophy of IDIC – 'Infinite Diversity in Infinite Combination' – from the original *Star Trek* series.[15] The CAW was formally chartered as a religion in the United States on 4 March 1968 – the first Earth-based religion, and the first hyper-real religion, to be so formally and legally recognised. Although the CAW was officially dissolved in 2004, Zell and the CAW have continued to play an influential role in neo-paganism to this day.

It should also be noted that the entirety of the neo-pagan set of beliefs has continued to be heavily influenced by fiction. There has always been a certain amount of mythic back-and-forth between fiction written by pagans and the practices of their faith – from the heavily neo-pagan influenced Marion Zimmer Bradley novel *The Mists of Avalon* (which many cite as their gateway text to the possibility of actually practicing paganism)[16] to Brian Bates' fictional interpretation of Celtic and Norse myth, *The Way Of Wyrd*,[17] to the rise of other openly pagan authors as major writers in the modern fantasy genre.[18]

Another immensely influential stream of the hyper-real was opened in the 1970s by the prolific writer and occultist, Kenneth

Grant (1924-2011). Grant, who was a friend of Crowley in his twilight years and was also the sole reason the work of proto- chaos magician Austin Osman Spare (1886-1956) was not lost after Spare's death in near-forgotten poverty, was a huge influence on modern occultism – not least because of his major role in the revival, and mystical interpretation, of the cosmic horror fiction of H.P. Lovecraft (1890-1937).

In a series of books now known as the Typhonian Trilogies, beginning with *The Magical Revival*,[19] Grant set out his theory that Lovecraft's Cthulhu Mythos stories were actually based on a genuine occult tradition, which Lovecraft had accessed subconsciously. This is of course highly debatable... nonetheless, a resurgence of interest in Lovecraft's work arose at the time, and the fictional lines were blurred even further with the publication of several books purporting to be the unexpurgated texts of the Cthulhu Mythos's key (and, according to Lovecraft, entirely fictional) occult tome, *The Necronomicon* – including one version which was partly ghost-written by the great British philosopher of the occult, Colin Wilson (1931-2013).[20]

Lovecraft's work and the Cthulhu Mythos are now so deeply intertwined into pop culture that they have indirectly influenced or directly led to games, films, associated novels[21] and comic books[22] ... and a range of surprisingly adorable plushy toys.

Grant's attitude to the adaptability of fiction as (at minimum) an inspiration for mysticism was a major influence on the school of occult practice known as chaos magic, which first appeared in the mid-1970s and has become a key influence on both the practice of applied mysticism and a great deal of modern fantasy literature (especially in the urban fantasy sub-genre) that has followed. Although Possamai does not interrogate chaos magic directly in his work, it is clearly (and usually explicitly) a postmodern magical system, and thus a thriving aspect of the hyper-real religious current.

The 1970s were a remarkably fecund time for the hyper-real religions – not least for the considerable growth in what has become known as the New Age Movement. Possamai regards this aspect of popular mysticism as an offshoot of the Human Potential Movement, whose roots Possamai traces to the 'sensitivity training' of the 1940s,[23] and which found wider acceptance in the 1960s. Although the Human Potential Movement was at its core a secular and humanistic one, aspects of its philosophy of deliberately-directed self-improvement of humanity filtered into the stream of imported Eastern spiritual ideas in the 1960s, becoming part of a popularised 'transcendence' narrative.

The various forms of New Age spirituality – ranging from the less explicitly mystical forms (such as EST and biofeedback training and the positive thinking/self-help practices ranging from Neuro-Linguistic Programming to *The Secret*[24]) to the more outright occult-tinged flavours ('White Light' paganism, pastel-coloured-angel worship etc) – have a common denominator... they are mass-produced, heavily marketed and designed with as much of an eye to commerce as to any personal enlightenment they may lead to. They are Product. And in that regard, they are perhaps the exemplary hyper-real religious practice.[25]

Possamai notes of the New Age adherent:

> They consume products for gaining and enhancing sensations. They can visit a 'New Age' healing centre for a few days, participate in a 'vision quest' and be initiated into shamanism, buy crystals and indigenous paraphernalia, learn astronomy... These objects for sale - books, tarot cards, crystals, CDs, aromatherapy products - have long lost any taint of the demonic and have become common products.[26]

After noting the dichotomy between the New Age 'hyper-consumer' beliefs (where individual choice is celebrated) and the 'hypo-consumerist' Fundamentalist beliefs (in which, although they are still believed by a community of consumers, the adherents have their consumption choices dictated by a hierarchical authority - more on these later), Possamai says of the New Age Movement:

> ...they are the consumer religion *par excellence*...

and,

> In traditional religions, the demand for religious objects is focussed
> on their authenticity. New objects will not be bought unless there
> is proof they are authentic for a specific religion, and that they
> contain the power of a specific source. In New Age, the individual
> is the main source of meaning attribution, and the authority of the
> object rests in the individual's decision and/or feeling about the
> worth of its religiousness.[27]

Possamai sub-divides the New Age beliefs - always a very wide blanket term, to be sure - into three flavours:

- *Aquarian Perrenism* – as in The Age Of..., "a modern movement valorising the future and progress" (expressions of this current range from the self-help movements noted above to the techno-futurist Transhumanism movement),
- *Neo-Paganism* – "an anti-modern movement valorising traditions, mainly pagan" (though I would note factors such as the bleed-over from sources such as the CAW mentioned above), and, of the greater significance to this piece,
- *Presentist Perrenism* – "a movement which has its genesis in post-modernity".

Possamai defines Presentist Perrenism further by saying that;

> ...even though it borrows eclectively from earlier esotericism, (it)
> is to be understood as an expression, in the field of spirituality, of
> emergent post-industrial or post-modern culture.[28]

By 'Perrenism' Possamai means a syncretic (drawing from many combined sources) spirituality which...

> ...interprets the world as *Monistic* (the cosmos is perceived as
> having its elements deeply interrelated. It recognises a single
> ultimate principle, being, or force, underlying all reality, and
> rejects the notion of dualism, e.g. mind/body);

> ...whose actors are attempting to develop their *Human Potential
> Ethic* (actors work on themselves for personal growth);

> ...and whose actors are seeking *Spiritual Knowledge* (the way to
> develop oneself is through a pursuit of knowledge, be it knowledge
> of the universe or of the self, the two being sometimes interrelated).[29]

It is this Presentist Perrenism that describes the fictional-sourced-or-influenced belief systems which are my primary interest here.

THE NEW GODS

"A Jedi must have the deepest commitment, the most serious mind...
Excitement. Adventure. A Jedi craves not these things"
– Yoda, in *The Empire Strikes Back*

One especially fruitful area of Possamai's study – and one whose significance has grown considerably since he first explored it – is the religious current deriving from *Star Wars*. Ever since the release of the first film in 1977, the *Star Wars* mythos has spoken to many people as a powerful expression of the ineffable – on a metaphorical level at least, the tales of the Jedi Knights and their use of the cosmic energy of The Force has connected with literally millions.

In the original creation of the *Star Wars* internal mythology (an ironic side-effect of George Lucas being unable to secure the rights to a *Flash Gordon* reboot), Lucas drew on many aspects of Eastern religion – Buddhism, Taoism and Shinto in particular – to build the mystical system practiced by the Jedi Knights. In a sense, this was an act of pure unadulterated cultural appropriation by a middle-class white boy from Orange County, California... but he was approaching these sources through the already assimilated New Age versions, and the resulting mix took on a life of its own. There's a directly appealing pull to the simplified version of Taoist dualism in his image of the Light and Dark sides of The Force...

> The Force is what gives a Jedi his power. It's an energy field created by all living things. It surrounds us and penetrates us. It binds the galaxy together.

Here, of course, Lucas is describing Ki/ch'i/mana/prana etc. by another name.

The other key aspect of how Lucas handled his burgeoning mythos was the work of Joseph Campbell, especially his development of the Monomyth concept.[30] Lucas hit every beat of Campbell's guide to tales of a mythological hero's journey with a ruthless efficiency – and it worked supremely well.

Of his creation, Lucas later said:

> I see *Star Wars* as taking all the issues that religion represents and trying to distil them down into a more modern and easily accessible construct... I put The Force into the movie in order to try and

Star Wars-related 'cosplay' at DragonCon 2006
(Image by Michael Neel, reprinted under Creative Commons Share-Alike licence)

awaken a certain kind of spirituality in young people – more of a belief in God than a belief in any particular religious system. I wanted to make it so that young people would begin to ask questions about the mystery... I didn't want to invent a religion.[31]

Clearly, Lucas succeeded - perhaps more than he ever intended. Right from the start, there were an awful lot of people who simply and truly wanted to learn the ways of the Force and become a Jedi. The rise of the internet allowed the earliest signs of this fervent wish to begin coalescing into an actual faith... but it was not until 2001 that this loose belief in The Force undertook a significant shift, both for itself and for hyper-real religion in general.

In that year the U.K., Australia, New Zealand and Canada undertook a national census, the first in which those surveyed were asked to state their religion. In the U.K. and Australia in particular, there was an enthusiastic internet-based campaign to encourage people to claim Jedi as their religion of choice. This was a remarkable success – *390,000 U.K. citizens* and over 70,000 Australians were now, officially, members of the Jedi faith. These figures made the Jedi faith *the fourth largest in the United Kingdom* – far ahead of Judaism and all of the non-Mosaic Eastern faiths, and considerably higher than the number of either Pagan or Scientology adherents. Of course, many of those claiming Jedi as their faith probably did so for a laugh, or to make a statement on the ridiculousness of having a religious census question in the first place... but some of them meant it. And, after receiving a substantial amount of publicity as a result, the wider public awareness of what was now becoming known as Jediism grew.[32]

Many online groups attempted to formalise the belief set (and, obviously, make allowances for the fact that adherents did not develop any notable Force-based superpowers). Their statements clearly show the syncretic and perrenist aspects of the belief. An example:

Jediism is not fiction. Our ways are based on ancient wisdom as well as modern philosophies. Our ways are modern adaptations of Taoism and Buddhism. We encourage activities that cultivate physical and mental health, such as martial arts and meditation.

Jediism is a philosophy above all. Then, we use the Order to get together, to stay in touch, to share our united view of life and the Force. It is not required to be a warrior to be a member of the Order of the Jedi, nor to be religiously implicated.

We are non-exclusive. This means that you may keep participating in the religion of your choice, and study the principles of the Force, with no obligations. Our members are free thinkers, with free minds.[33]

The drive for Jediism to be recognised as the equal to any other non-hyper-real belief system won some major successes, especially in the UK. In 2005, newly elected Member of Parliament Jaimie Reed was seated as the first stated member of the Jedi in the House of Commons (although he later confessed to having done so as a joke and as a comment on a religious freedoms bill being then debated).[34] In 2006, two Jedi delivered a protest letter to the United Nations in recognition of the International Day of Tolerance.[35] In 2009, it became known that eight serving police officers in Scotland's Strathclyde force identified as Jedi.[36]

In 2010, an interesting comparison appeared between the treatment of hyper-real religions versus the more established faiths. It began when a self-identified Jedi walked into a British Job Centre. When asked to lower his hood, he politely refused, saying that keeping his hood raised was an article of his faith. He was asked to leave for 'security reasons'. After submitting a formal complaint to the Department of Work and Pensions, he received a written apology from the branch manager. Around the same time, a Christian nurse lost her law suit against her employers at the National Health Service for being forced to conceal her crucifix at work.[37] Although U.K. law has specifically ruled against Jedi having the same religious entitlements as other faiths (along with Satanists, those who preach female genital mutilation and Scientologists – a delightful comparison),[38] in practice it is not only holding its own with orthodox religion, but can clearly on occasion be given even greater respect.

It should also be noted that the late capitalistic aspects of Jediism-as-product are considerable. Not only the quantity of material, but the quality (replica lightsabers have come a *long* way in 37 years!) and sheer ease of availability of physical manifestations of the mythos are both a continual manifestation of that belief and a multi-billion dollar industry (and, as any religionist will tell you, nothing makes a belief more concrete for the faithful than having physical objects which represent it). The upcoming resurgence of *Star Wars* product as a result of the sale of the franchise to the Disney Corporation – themselves an exemplar of the hyper-real in Baudrillard's eyes[39] – will likely lead to still further growth of Jediism.

Jediism may be the best known of the purely fictional-based beliefs, but there are many others: Matrixism (deriving from the mythos of the *Matrix* films) and the Na'vi mysticism of James Cameron's film *Avatar*, for example. There are also the satirical or spoof religions – Discordianism,[40] The Church of the SubGenius, The Church of the Flying Spaghetti Monster etc. – whose adherents of appropriately varying sincerity have claimed their own space in culture and even law, further blurring the lines of what can be considered a 'true faith'.

Some people have taken such hyper-real beliefs even further and hold that *their very souls* are a manifestation of the fictional into our realm. These folk, who call themselves Otherkin, have existed for quite some time (I became personally acquainted with several people who believed their true souls were essentially Tolkienesque elves as early as the mid-1980s), but the term is of fairly recent origin – and, of course, the internet has allowed them to more easily 'find the others'. Despite the considerable scorn of many, they have found a strength and consistency in their non-human soul models – although there are controversies within their ranks, mostly around a schism between the majority who hold to a non-specific species of soul origin (elf, wolf, dragon etc) and those who believe they are specific reincarnations of fictional entities (such as Neo of *The Matrix* or one of many anime characters).[41] It would seem that no religion is immune to fractioning.

BACKLASH

"Life doesn't work like stories."
- Blue, in *Six-Gun Gorilla*[42]

As I noted earlier, Possamai's studies have not been limited to the 'presentist perrenist', fiction-embracing faiths. The Yang to the Yin of these post-modern beliefs is what Possamai calls the 'hypo-consumerist' element of modern religion: how the already existing faiths have striven to co-opt, dilute or utterly oppose the influence of popular culture on their adherents.

These reactions vary widely. The more extremist forces (usually of the Mosaic religions) include such aggressive displays as a variety of Islamic *fatwas* against various popular materials (usually condemned for their 'Western' origin as much as for their heterodox content) and the book and record burnings so beloved of the American Christian right. Other branches of traditional faiths attempt to draw on popular currents to further their aims. These range from the use of comic books and popular literature used to directly preach (such as the long-standing Jack Chick comics[43]) to the resurgence in Christian-oriented works (such as the phenomenally successful *Left Behind* franchise), movies like *The*

Passion of the Christ (2004), the recent wave of exorcism-related films, and the substantial production line of Christian-oriented music in various genres.

Many modern preachers (especially those in the 'megachurch' ministries, which, Possamai has noted, increasingly resemble shopping malls) are quite comfortable to purloin aspects of pop culture in their sermons, while of course never quite straying over the line into considering those sources as actually having any spiritual worth of their own. Others (such as Rabbi Cary Friedman, author of the delightful *Wisdom from the Batcave*[44]) can find confirmation and inspiration for their own faith within works of pop culture. Between condemnation and co-option, the orthodox faiths strive to keep the encroaching wave of modernism (and, far worse, postmodernism) at bay, with varying levels of success even within their own ranks.

Aside from the resistance from the older, orthodox faiths, there are of course specific issues in regard to the hyper-real religions and their place within the realm of contemporary belief systems. Bluntly put: if you are able to accept a fictional origin for your spirituality, what happens when you apply that to the real world? And, in such cases... how much is too much?

Here is an example of what happens when somebody takes their hyper-real beliefs rather too stringently to heart. Around British science fiction fandom in the 1980s, there was a woman who was an enthusiastic participant of the occult/pagan fringe which so often overlaps SF&F fandom. Her preferred personal mythos was Pern – the planet of telepathically-bonded dragon-riding heroes in the books of Anne McCaffrey. As you can imagine, when this person finally got to meet Ms. McCaffrey herself, it was quite an important moment... one which she spent explaining in excruciating detail to McCaffrey what the author and the books had got wrong about Pern, on the basis that *she had been there via the Astral Plane and knew better.*

(Of course, the possibility that she was right about Pern has to be mentioned... anyone who's familiar with Alan Moore's theory of Idea-Space[45] could raise the possibility that there is an Ur-Pern out there in the imaginal realm, and that some folk could conceivably make contact with it. Or even that Pern, faults and all, truly does physically exist somewhere in deep space and she actually did pick up some telepathic vibe coming from it, or even translated her soul there in some manner. Nonetheless; going up to the person who is pretty sure they actually invented that world with overriding declarations of your version of their invented reality as utter truth is, at bare minimum, impolite and just plain tacky.)

Alan Moore

This story illustrates what I think is the most important factor in not just the hyper-real beliefs, but adherence to any religious text or mythos in general – the importance of treating metaphor *as metaphor*. The disparity between the stories our culture tells and the actually existing subjects (simulations rather than simulacra, in Baudrillard's terminology) of those stories can often be distinguished when the subject is deeply at odds with the story.

Consider the dissonance when watching a fictional version of a subject or profession you have some expertise in and the version on your screen. Or note how the ubiquity of fantasy versions of forensic science in TV shows such as the *CSI* franchise has led to a massively skewed public perception of the capabilities of that science – to the point that lawyers complain about the influence of 'CSI Syndrome' on juries' perception of evidence in cases.[46] The smarter hyper-real religionist should always be aware that, no matter how hard postmodernist and poststructuralist theory may insist, confusing story with fact has consequences – possibly severe ones. (As I often say, after Austin Spare – treat your spiritual perceptions and inclinations *as if* they are real, not *as* real.) But, within one's own mythos or set of metaphors, many truths may be found – for a given value of 'truth'.

All of this came to a head recently, in a case which horrified the world and brought the hyper-real very directly into the Real.

The attempted murder of a 12 year old girl in Wakuesha, Wisconsin by two of her classmates, as a sacrifice to summon the favour of the internet-birthed monster Slenderman,[47] made it very clear that a creature of a known fictional origin could be the (alleged) inspiration for crimes just as vicious as any perpetrated by fanatics of a conventional religion. News media seized on the story – some offering it as an example of the pernicious influence of the internet on children, others considering the overall role of story and myth on modern humanity. With two other Slenderman influenced cases (one involving the murder of two policemen in Las Vegas[48]) mere days before the fifth anniversary of Slenderman's creation, it seemed that a point of no return had been reached. One might almost consider 31 May 2014 as the 9/11 of the hyper-real – after that date, nothing will quite be the same again.[49]

CONCLUSION

> "We read books to find out who we are. What other people, real
> or imaginary, do and think and feel... is an essential guide to our
> understanding of what we ourselves are and may become."
> - Ursula K. Le Guin

Possamai's terminology – hyper-real religion, presentist perrenism – provides a useful perspective on a rising aspect of modern belief, one which manages to bring some clarity as to why people can derive spiritual guidance from one or more of the many fictional tales which permeate modern culture. It may even point the way to a position

'The Slenderman'. Image courtesy Cachét Whitman (pirate-cashoo.deviantart.com)

which rides the constantly shifting tides of that culture without either descending into Future Shock or surrendering to the particularly whiny form of nihilism that the non-spiritual postmodern adherents are often inclined to.

The hyper-real religionist (unless they simply take on a single belief system such as Jediism) draws on a smorgasbord of metaphorical possibilities, integrating these perspectives into how they self-define their personality... and as long as those metaphors have a personal resonance, their origin matters not at all. The Presentist Perrenist is, by nature, comfortable with a much higher degree of epistemological uncertainty than a monoculturalist practitioner – often, they have been disappointed by the lack of connection the more orthodox faiths have with the modern condition and look wider afield for something that can provide a connection to their own life experiences. The myths of our times can provide a wide and varied pantheon of heroic figures to draw on for comfort and inspiration – as Christopher Knowles put it so well in the title of his book on the modern mythology of comics, 'Our Gods Wear Spandex'.[50]

A criticism many would make of these perspectives is that the hyper-real religions are nothing more than a manifestation of the saturation of culture by mass-produced product. I would say that, although this is a factor, there is more often than not a spirit of self-adaptation, of *bricolage*, a guerilla-like use of the products of late capitalism against themselves, to the practice – a rich inventiveness which combines the love of stories manifest in the best of culture (fannish and otherwise) with the hopes, experiences and aspirations of genuine spiritual seekers. The act of absorbing and respecting aspects of so many variant stories may indeed allow them to find a more egalitarian, multi-modal perspective on faith and belief – a positive manifestation of what orthodox religionists so often sneer at as "pick-and-mix spirituality".

There may even be a greater honesty in admitting one's religious metaphors come from an invented source rather than making unprovable claims to any kind of historical 'authenticity'... as long as those metaphors never harden into dogma. Although, as the Wisconsin incident clearly showed, one must be as careful in regards to the pernicious effects of fanaticism and absolute belief with the hyper-real beliefs as with the traditional ones.

In terms of religious belief, these manifestations have a short history, barely half a century. But they are becoming a growing part of the conversation about how we view the Divine, and will open new possibilities for those disappointed by the Old Gods and the old certainties.

"The entire universe appears to be a huge theatre of mirrors in which every object hides a secret, in which everything is a sign that hides mystery."

– Adam Possamai

Ian 'Cat' Vincent was born on Imbolc-Groundhog Day in 1964. He is a lifelong student of the occult, and a former professional combat magician and curse-breaker. His writing on Forteana and magic, especially on the magical approach he terms 'Guttershaman', can be found at http://catvincent.com. Cat is a feature writer for *Fortean Times,* as well as being a columnist for http://spiralnature.com. He lives in Yorkshire, England with his wife, the artist and writer Kirsty Hall. He is often found on Twitter as @catvincent.

His favourite deities are Babalon, Eris, Ganesha and Valen from Babylon 5.

TOO DEEP!

FOR ORDINARY MAN

The strange history of the Shaver Mystery craze

by *Blair MacKenzie Blake*

"The world is sure full of crackpots!" bellowed the associate editor after reading aloud for laughs portions of a letter addressed to the offices of the pulp science fiction magazine *Amazing Stories*. As with previous specimens from cranks, he crushed the nonsensical ramblings into a ball and tossed it into the wastebasket. Hearing these remarks through the intervening wall, the magazine's editor-in-chief – a diminutive hunchbacked figure with a normally cheerful disposition and decidedly puckish sense of humor – got up from his desk and retrieved the letter from the garbage. Smoothing out the crumpled paper, he saw that it contained details of an intergalactic alphabet that the sender considered to be an "immensely important find", in that it constituted undeniable proof of the Atlantean legend. Conducting a few casual experiments with this universal language called Mantong (Earth's "mother tongue"), while repeatedly applying the formula of the root words' hidden meaning, the results proved interesting. Whether merely on a lark, or to show who was the boss; he chided his friend for a lack of editorial judgment, and told him to run the entire letter in the next issue. In doing so, on that winter's day in 1943, the orbits of two remarkable men would soon cross, and with their combined efforts, they were about to create a publishing sensation.

SHAVERMANIA

The energetic young editor of *Amazing Stories*, Ray Palmer, was on a mission to take his pulp adventures to the next level. To attract a

Ray Palmer

wider audience, he would need to blur the boundaries of his cliché-ridden space operas, or at least combine their flashy trappings with more esoteric concepts. After presenting the strange letter in the January 1944 issue, the response was both positive and negative, but because there was such a large response, he sensed that he had tapped into something really big. In the letter that he salvaged, the writer hinted that he knew much more about this antediluvian super-civilization, and that to keep the incredible truth from dying with him, all he needed was a little encouragement.

And encourage him Palmer did, with a letter requesting additional information. What he got in return was a ten-thousand-word hodge-podge entitled "A Warning To Future Man." Although the 'submission' was of poor literary quality and possibly the work of a raving lunatic, Palmer was fascinated by the basic premise.

The only problem was that the author – a factory worker from Pennsylvania named Richard (Sharpe) Shaver – claimed that the story was true, and *Amazing Stories* was strictly a fiction magazine. Coming up with a solution, Palmer re-crafted the manuscript, correcting the grammatical atrocities, and re-titled it "I Remember Lemuria!" To lessen the concerns that his bosses had about this new mutation, he informed his readers that it was an incredible example of "racial memory" by its courageous author. The response was better than anyone at the offices of the Ziff-Davis publishing empire could

Richard Shaver

ever have imagined. Letters poured in by the hundreds and sales skyrocketed.

Just as surprising as the boost in circulation were the letters from readers sharing their personal experiences of Shaver's bizarre accounts involving the degenerative remnants of humanity's glorious heritage. In a special section called "Report from the Forgotten Past", these letters included encounters with malignant entities by cave explorers, memories of previous incarnations, disembodied voices, and other inexplicable phenomena. With each new installment of "The Shaver Mystery", Palmer challenged his readers to get involved in order to either prove or disprove Shaver's wild claims. In hyping Shaver's "thought-records" of ancient Lemuria, he not only had to stoke the fire of die-hard believers, but also had to deal with the wrath from fandom – those science fiction purists who accused him of perverting the genre by promoting Shaver's hokum. Amid the controversy, as copies of *Amazing Stories* were snatched up from newsstands, Palmer received a bump in salary, as did Shaver whose rate increased to two cents per word.

Spot Welder and Star Mech

"There is no way to tell you but incoherently – so I will do it
that way." – Richard Shaver

How it all really began may never be known as the story has morphed
over time. Shaver himself admitted that his memory had blurred, or
more likely that certain things were erased by invisible rays beamed
at his brain by those who wanted to discredit him, thereby allowing
the hideous depravity of their chthonic playgrounds to remain
secret. This tampering of his mind could account for many of the
inconsistent and often contradictory elements in the mystery, but if
we are to believe at least one version of Shaver's story, it started back
in 1932 when he was employed as a spot welder for the original Ford
Motor plant in Highland Park, Michigan.

One day while working on the assembly line he heard voices, "far
off voices of endless complexity." Noting that this occurred while
holding a certain welding gun, he rationalized that "by some freak of
its coils' field attunement" the tool had become a 'teleradio'." During
another shift, the incoherent babble became clearer, with voices
that "somehow didn't sound quite human." Even more disturbing,
he heard the anguished screams of a woman along with monstrous
snuffles. What he was hearing – or, rather, the impressions that he
was receiving in his head – was the horrible satisfaction of sickening
creatures torturing human females that had been abducted from
the surface. Through this "thought augmenter", he also heard the
mentioning of ancient space-vessels.

Having stuffed his ears with cotton, the tormenting voices and
maniacal laughter continued. Unable to ignore the cruelty and the
misery, but mainly concerned about what was happening in the dark
recesses of his mind, he quit his job and went on the bum. While
tramping about in Depression-era America, at one point, Shaver was
either locked away in jail or admitted to a mental hospital.

Whichever it was, while held in confinement, one night "she first appeared to me like a vision... a mere ghost or dream that has drifted over to linger briefly in the real world."

Shaver called the enticing dream-woman Nydia, and her repeated presence in his cell filled him with delicious sensations of pleasure. At times, when looked at from different angles, her intense luminosity became hazy and colorless, which made him realize that she was a visual projection of some kind. On one of her frequent visits, a dazed, unseeing guard whose mind was obviously being controlled by a powerful beam technology released Shaver from his prison. With the solid illusion of Nydia taking his hand, the two hurried down the corridor and escaped into the wooded countryside. After traveling for miles, they entered a cleverly disguised cavern.

Standing on an ancient polished floor, Nydia abruptly disappeared, only to be replaced by the flesh and blood real thing. This blind woman was one of the secret-people, and as a direct descendent of an alien race, she would restore Shaver's sanity by divulging to him a mysterious realm of unfathomable complexity that had for millennia existed in tandem with an unsuspecting humanity. While in the cavern-world, amid great halls filled with "televiewer-screens" and the dizzying activity of endlessly varied machines, he experienced a sense of timelessness: "Time had lost all meaning... We were walking between the ticks of a clock, in a world ever suspended in the right now." Witnessing this still operable treasure-house of mechanization, Shaver took mental notes of the metallic enigmas, and eventually came to understand how these technological artifacts of the gods' underground exile were now being used as terrible weapons focused on the surface world.

The historical record that Shaver was told concerned a race of super-beings that had migrated from their home in the far reaches of interstellar space and colonized the earth many thousands of years ago. In the dim glimmering of persistent legends, these nearly immortal, resplendent humanoids were known collectively as the Elder gods.

In their pristine new surroundings, the advanced civilizations of the Titans and Atlans flourished for countless centuries until the sun gradually began to change. Bombarded by poisonous solar radiation, in a desperate attempt to stave off its degenerative effects, they artificially hollowed out vast cavernous cities. When this proved fruitless, they decided to once again search for a new home amongst the stars.

With limited transport on their great space-liners, the less fortunate were left behind, including the artificial race that they genetically fashioned to enforce their will. Some of these primitive creations (the ancestors of modern humans) returned to the surface and adjusted to the harmful energy. Others didn't, and continued to devolve in their subterranean empire. Shaver called these mutated horrors the "dero" (a contraction of the words "detrimental robot"), with their more benign fellow cavern dwellers known as the "tero" (short for "integrative robot"). In the case of the former, at least, the word "robot" meant that they had "no real self-control of their actions."

Even in their regressed state, both the dero and tero still had access to the marvelous inventions abandoned by the long-departed Elder gods, and throughout the ages the dero had used these machines (which Shaver termed "mech") to torment humankind. Although the tero attempt to thwart the dero's twisted desires, to these psychotic gnomes humans were but toys for sexual frenzies, and yet another species of edible animal. Besides the mind-staggering debauchery in their squalid lairs, with their mastery of the powerful ray-mech they created constant mayhem, and were solely responsible for all of the evil that plagues the human population (being the foundation of the Biblical devil and hell). This included everything from spontaneous human combustion to someone slipping on a banana peel. If a mother drowned her baby, the voices in her head that told her to do so were beamed from the caverns of the dero. Likewise with the assassination of a political figure, or even a child getting his kicks by pulling the wings off of flies. To Shaver, any attempt on man's part to defeat the dero would prove futile, so long as they possessed the ancient mech.

Nydia or Nurse?

Years after 'The Shaver Mystery' faded into obscurity, Palmer would constantly be asked if the whole thing was an elaborate hoax perpetrated by its co-creators in order to make a quick buck. Although he always denied such accusations, in a later publication he divulged that that during the entire duration that Shaver claimed to be in the caverns, he was actually in various mental institutions, including a lengthy stay (1938-1943) at the Ionia State Hospital for the Criminally Insane after being diagnosed with paranoid schizophrenia. In light of these revelations, could the dream-woman Nydia have been in reality one of the overcrowded asylum's more compassionate psychiatric nurses? When Shaver wrote that the dero's insanity "only seemed to enhance their creative instinct to find new and different ways to inflict torture upon [him]," was he really describing the doctors' experiments with metrazol convulsion and transcranial electroshock procedures? If so, then the "telaug" and other terrible influencing beams responsible for scrambling his neural-circuitry might well have been the current from the electroshock apparatus that was used on him while under restraint. It should also be noted that shock treatments such as these could cause retrograde amnesia, which might explain the time distortion and memory lapses that Shaver experienced. To those who had long suggested that Shaver was mentally unbalanced, Palmer proposed the other side of the coin, asking his sci-fi brethren to consider that if the dero really were tampering with his mind via invisible ray trickery, then wouldn't that prompt him to seek psychiatric care? Indeed, that the asylums were filled with patients in similar catatonic states only proved the validity of the Shaver Mystery!

Vestiges of the Bicameral Mind?

With the surplus of Shaver's writings that Palmer had after "The Most Sensational True Story Ever Told" disappeared from the pages of *Amazing Stories*, in the early 1960s he cobbled together these personal letters and raw submissions into a sixteen-volume monument to Shaverdom entitled *The Hidden World*.

Now that the truth could finally be told, Shaver hinted about his time at Ionia, stating that the tale of the mental institution "has just enough truth at the back of it to make it embarrassing." He also admitted that he had been hearing voices inside his head long before his experiences with the welding gun at the auto plant. So perhaps he was just a nut job after all? In all likelihood his sloppily-typed techno-erotic obsessions might have been forever destined to the circular file were it not for Palmer's skillful hand at re-molding them, combined with his carnival barker-like showmanship. Or could there actually be some reality behind Shaver's "mother-tongue" alphabet and the Elder gods who genetically created (or modified) the human race before their exodus in remote antiquity?

The answer to both Shaver's original language (Mantong) and the intrusive voices in his head might have some grounding in psychologist Julian Jaynes' revolutionary thesis that human consciousness is a learned process that at some point manifested into being out of an earlier hallucinatory mentality. In his book *The Origins of Consciousness in the Breakdown of the Bicameral Mind* (1976), Jaynes contends that perhaps as recently as 3000 years ago humans lacked self-awareness and instead experienced auditory hallucinations or commands from the gods that initiated their behavior. After the transition into subjective consciousness that we know today, vestiges of the bicameral state can still be detected, with one being acute schizophrenia. For Jaynes, the idea of external gods giving guidance to unknowing automatons is a metaphor for the cognitive functions of our divided brain.

Cover of *The Hidden World*, Spring 1961: "The True Story of The Shaver Mystery"

But what if the gods *were* actually advanced beings from elsewhere (as opposed to the allegorical workings of the central nervous system), who genetically tailored humankind and hard-wired their new creation to be obedient to internal voice commands? If traces of the Elders' programmed commands still occurred in some people, then this detrimental neurological tampering could account for both Shaver's ancient thought-records and the nefarious activity of the dero, with the latter being a sporadic corruption of normal introspection. Granted, this is a big "if", to what otherwise might simply be considered one social outcast's wacky beliefs.

Dero, Mantong, Tero

One other stone that perhaps should not be left unturned is the notion that the induced seizures of electroconvulsive therapy altered Shaver's brain chemistry and possibly released trace amounts of endogenous tryptamines. Modern recreational users of exogenous DMT and other psychoactive substances might compare Shaver's descriptions of the dero as "fearfully anemic jitterbugs" and "goggled-eyed wizened-imps" with their own encounters with 'self-transforming machine elves'. Extravagant machinery such as that described in the caverns of the tero and dero have also been glimpsed while exploring the mostly uncharted tryptamine-enriched realms, with another common reoccurring theme being a lost or alien language that the gaggle of fractal entities attempt to teach to intrepid psychonauts. Although most people who experiment with entheogens like DMT find themselves launched into an intensely colorful and vastly more complex reality, for the most part, the adventure is a pleasurable (albeit shocking) one. However, there are many reports of negative experiences in which the tryptanaut is made to feel unwelcome by the evil jesters that inhabit this 'hyperspace'.

It could also be that once a person enters this fantastically ornate frame, the trans-spatial puppets there to greet them are merely a distraction from what really lies behind the immense vistas of gleaming, prismatic palaces. Even so, the problem with this scenario is that the tryptamine-induced mindscape actually seems far stranger than the nightmarish grandeur of Shaver's underground colonies, whose troglodyte pleasure stim-dens appear more like a funhouse mirror-warped neon-splashed Trocadero burlesque. (Interestingly enough, using Shaver's Mantong alphabet, "Trocadero" translates to "tero-see-a-dero.") As depicted on *Amazing Stories'* garish cover illustrations, Shaver's ancient yet futuristic tableau of heroic, bronze-hued inhabitants, with their jeweled ray-mech, gyroscopic devices with flashing lights, and hulking, ponderous torpedo-shaped trams is the stuff that the early pulp authors envisioned as science in its fullest bloom, and not the scarcely imagined terrain of DMT. Although we can't completely rule out endogenous tryptamines, it would appear that Shaver's hidden world just isn't weird enough.

Artificial Caverns or Ethereal Plateaus?

As mentioned earlier, after the Shaver Mystery had run its course, Palmer's continued response to his pulpster critics – even with all the fanzine parodies and boycotts – was that Shaver was not consciously perpetrating a hoax, but genuinely believed in the underground world. The Shaver Mystery was a collaborative effort, in which he (Palmer) added the "trimmings" to Shaver's first-hand accounts of the strange happenings. Yet, there was one bone of contention that would remain throughout their lives. Shaver was a firm materialist, who insisted that the loathsome "abandondero" were flesh and blood creatures, while Palmer, on the other hand, harbored spiritualist beliefs. Many of these occult notions were based on the channeled writings in *Oahspe*, the new-revelationist bible that was allegedly

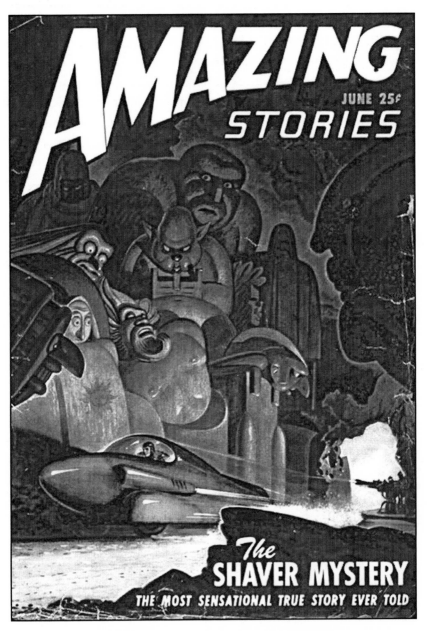

The 'All Shaver' Issue of *Amazing Stories*, June 1947

produced by automatic writing in 1882. In Palmer's worldview, rather than dwelling beneath the earth's surface, both the tero and dero were spirits of the dead that inhabit the various ethereal plateaus that encompass our planet. Having made little moral advancement while alive on the earth, in their other-vibratory nature, the dero still delight in evil as they roam the lower astral planes. Because Shaver's belief system rejected the séances of trance mediums or just about anything of a mystical nature, he countered that even the spiritually-degraded dead don't eat their human delicacies after roasting them on a spit. When asked, himself, if he was actually in the caverns and not merely dreaming them, he steadfastly maintained that he was, adding, "every time I pinched myself, it hurt."

Whatever their true nature might be, the dero's eagerness to wreak havoc among the surface people soon had them focusing their controlling rays on Ray Palmer's Chicago offices. While preparing an issue of *Amazing Stories* that was devoted entirely to the Shaver Mystery, the normally routine process was fraught with problems. Not only did galleys mysteriously disappear, the skilled typographers had found hundreds of spelling mistakes whereas the equally capable proofreaders hadn't found a single one. After a complete resetting of the all-Shaver issue (June, 1947), Palmer informed his readers that the dero had sabotaged the project in order to prevent the magazine from exposing the truth about their mad domain. (Indeed, the present author fears retribution from the little buggers in the form of grammatical mischief!)

Even though this was almost certainly another shameless promotion on the part of the chummy trickster, Palmer was becoming increasingly paranoid about certain going-ons in his little world. Not only was he questioning whether or not the dero were responsible for a recent series of accidents, he also wondered if they were the unseen forces behind a tragic childhood that left him crippled for life. Now as a seasoned editor who created the next wave in science 'fiction', he was the subject of ridicule by disgruntled fans who accused him of single-handedly destroying the genre with his "psi-fi." With the smear campaign in full force, he knew that the Shaver Mystery's days were numbered. Despite the increase in circulation, to the owners of *Amazing*, it was just too controversial. With all of the unflattering comments, it was also dangerous, as it tarnished their lucrative brand. Even worse, someone claimed that Shaver's science of the Elders contradicted Einstein's Theory of Relativity. By 1948, both *Amazing's* owners and Palmer were distancing themselves from Shaver's rampaging deros. Having "proved" to their satisfaction the reality of Shaver's ancient cavern world, Palmer informed its devoted followers that from here on out it would be up to a newly created "Shaver Mystery Club" to continue with the search for the truth. Any further Shaver stories would be labeled as "terrific yarns" (i.e. fiction).

FLYING SAUCERS BRING FRESH DESPAIR

Palmer was still smarting from the upstairs decision to discontinue his entertaining, provocative, and highly profitable inner earth series. True, his brilliant hunch had paid off, but now he needed something new that would spark the imagination of people. Almost seamlessly his readership provided the answer. At the same time that he was being ostracized for his heretical Shaver matters, in the letters that piled up in the mailroom, he noticed a growing interest in the new post-war phenomenon concerning mysterious flying objects moving at tremendous speeds. It didn't take Palmer (or Shaver) long to point out that these disc-ships were the same anti-gravitic flying machines called "Rollat" and "Zonton" that Shaver's Elder gods had piloted. Here again was something long predicted in the pages of pulp science fiction that had suddenly become a reality. Best of all, the wave of reports by witnesses all over the globe further proved Shaver's legitimate mystery. These unexplained flying objects would become Palmer's new obsession, and in his latest brainchild – a monthly publication entitled *Fate Magazine* – the sideshow huckster in him would tirelessly promote their baffling existence.

When asked about these disc-shaped craft, Shaver was a bit more pessimistic than his friend. To him the flying saucers only brought fresh despair. Some were merely "telesolidgraph" projections used as evasive tactics to protect the genuine article. Others were alien spacecraft drawn from the interstellar deeps to plunder and exploit a treasure that lies inside the earth, which these beings refer to as the Great Tomb. According to Shaver, they were not here to liberate us from the dero's control. Were they benevolent – wanting to free us from the ancient unseen chains – they would be destroyed by the hoarders of the mech. This is why they don't land on the White House lawn or attempt to communicate with the top brass at the Pentagon. In truth they are the very beings that left behind the now contaminated god-machines in a world beyond comprehension located right beneath our feet.

NOTHING NEW UNDER THE DETRIMENTAL SUN

Nowadays, Shaver enthusiasts are quick to remind us that his stories and articles in the 1940s contained many of the elements that are present in modern UFO lore. These include the ancient astronaut hypothesis, saucer-craft with gravity-deflecting devices, the crash-retrieval of alien vehicles, and the abduction of humans by otherworldly beings that visit the earth unsuspected. In the same issues of *Amazing* that featured the Shaver Mystery, the letters column was often filled with reports of similar UFO-related events. One of these was from a man named W.C. Hefferlin, who described sleek circle-winged planes that resembled a flattened cookie or doughnut before Kenneth Arnold's famous sighting in

June of 1947. Roswell aficionados might be interested to know that these spacecraft of Hefferlin's were constructed of self-healing materials, and had revolutionary, bowl-shaped propulsion drives. Also mentioned were peculiar metals that were lightweight and flexible and etched with symbols in some unknown tongue. Not out of the question is whether or not this letter/article was actually written by the impish Palmer himself? If so, perhaps to add a touch of realism, he took several editorial potshots at Hefferlin's claims in the magazine's next issue!

Of all the modern UFO accounts, one in particular seems to be rehashed from the Shaver Mystery. This is the high strangeness surrounding Archuleta Mesa in Dulce, New Mexico. This exceeding ominous place was once the epicenter of sightings of anomalous lights, cattle mutilations, phantom helicopters, and dark rumors of the abduction of humans by paraphysical entities. According to some witnesses, the rugged terrain of the Archuleta plateau conceals a multi-level underground facility that contains a joint government-alien biogenetic laboratory. On one of the levels, dubbed "Nightmare Hall", some of the most horrific bioengineering programs take place. Reports describe genetically modified creations suspended in tanks aglow with an eerie luminescence. Shaver buffs will recognize the similarity between these freakish things and the variform breeding by Atlantean technicons. If the reports about the Dulce installation are based in reality, then does this further validate Shaver's insistence that his stories were factual? Might the demented hordes with their stunted misshapen forms, pallid skin, and huge protruding eyes be one and the same with the hostile grey extraterrestrial biological entities that are believed by many to be involved with the abduction phenomenon? If this is the case, then these hybrid curiosities floating in vats of fluorescent proteins might be experiments involving polyembryony techniques conducted by the dero in an attempt to reverse their own genetic degradation.

Cover of *The Coming of the Saucers*, by Kenneth Arnold and Ray Palmer

Other similarities with the Dulce complex and Shaver's cavern world include massive drill borings to hollow out an extensive network of tunnels, tube shuttle connections, ventilated shafts, and hangars for stealthy aeroforms. As for the ancient mech, the modern day mind stalkers are purported to use an array of beam weaponry that includes Radio Hypnotic Intra-Cerebral Controls, 3D holographic projections, electronic dissolution of memory devices, and powerful scalar machinery. Unless certain sections of the preceding text were tampered with, most of these things should now sound familiar?

One letter in *Amazing Stories* sent by a returned soldier spoke of seeing his buddies being zapped by frightening little creatures with flash guns while they were rooting out Japanese troops hunkered down in caves on an island in the south Pacific. This brings to mind the much written about Dulce shoot out, where 'the Greys' allegedly used sophisticated beam weapons against military security personnel in order to seize control of one of the labs.

Although it is debatable whether either Shaver or Palmer should be credited with inventing flying saucers (as some have suggested), they certainly advanced many of the basic features associated with the phenomenon. In his subsequent publications, Palmer was definitely ahead of the curve when it came to the shadowy world of government cover-ups, fabled civilizations, occult masters, suppressed Nazi technology, and conspiracies involving the New World Order. It seems a shame that both men died prior to the theatrical release of *Close Encounters of the Third Kind*. In the film, the place chosen by the aliens to make contact with humans is "Devil's Tower" in Wyoming. To those who demanded proof of his outrageous claims, Shaver insisted that this national monument was actually an enormous petrified tree stump that remained from the days that the Titans roamed the earth. Of course, this and other fantastic things from the Golden Age are scattered all around us in the shattered pieces of an ancient repository of earth's secret history. One only needed to know how to properly view them...

TAMPERING WITH ROKFOGO

In the spring of 1960 Shaver made a discovery on his farm that would preoccupy him until his death in 1975. Finally he had tangible proof of the legends of our distant past. What appeared as ordinary rocks to the uninitiated were actually pre-deluge artifacts that Shaver called rokfogo (using the Mantong language). According to Shaver, slicing the agate into thin layers with a diamond saw revealed glimpses of the Atlantean civilization in its original splendor. However, intertwined with the jumble of beautiful portraits are the hideous faces of the dero – tampering with the picture books so as to keep us in the dark. To some, these ancient records of the Elders are nothing more than a case of pareidolia, similar to seeing pictures in cloud formations or images in the random patterns of linoleum swirls. Nevertheless, over time, using optical techniques and other crude methods, Shaver found a way of transferring the images imprinted on the rocks onto canvases. With the kaleidoscope of figures amid a phantasmagoria of dero activity, these paintings have recently been displayed in galleries as fine examples of Outsider Art. As to his new obsession, Shaver believed that his work might not be understood for centuries.

MADMAN OR FUTANT?

Those who knew Shaver in his later years describe him as being gentle and intelligent. If he wasn't sane in an insane world that was being controlled by an onslaught of antique weapon rays embedded deep inside the earth, then the question becomes: Did Shaver 'cure' his mental illness by using his high-powered imagination to create an alternate reality that could in effect explain the mocking voices and circus of death in his head?

Scientific notes containing detailed technical illustrations that were written by him while a patient at the Ionia State Hospital have survived. Having been scribbled on the back of hospital report forms, it seems likely that he was supplied with pencils by a nurse that he befriended during his long stay there.

But what about the bizarre sexual perversions that permeate Shaver's writings in scenes that are far more graphic (and revolting) than *Amazing's* cover art depictions of scantily clad space damsels receiving "stim" while stretched out on divans in their futuristic

domiciles? Anyone who has read Shaver's accounts of the dero's sadomasochistic torture sessions might welcome this literary delirium. Especially when someone else – if not having the mental means to slide their naked victims inexorably into gleaming machines that gradually sliced them into wafer-thin pieces - mutilated them instead with a butcher's knife. One might suppose that it would be easier not to obey the commands of voices in one's head knowing fully well that one's tormenters were "the worst possible result of what the human race could descend to."

Does it really take a semi-literate ex-steel worker who was a former insane asylum patient to tell us that WE are the dero (as well as the tero, who struggle to keep things in check)? With the proliferation of advanced technologies – including genetically engineered organisms, self-replicating machines, artificial intelligence and virtual reality possibilities – perhaps we should reevaluate Shaver's nonsensical ramblings. Rather than being "the most celebrated rumpus that rocked the science fiction world" (as *Life* magazine described it), or as the forerunner of X-Files-type fringe phenomena, the machines-gone-mad world of the dero might be closer to the surface than we were previously led to believe. As to his stories of ancient Lemuria, was

Shaver 'remembering' the future, asking us to consider the potential dire consequences of opening these Pandora's boxes? Were it not for the acute hearing of Ray Palmer, this warning to future man by a true visionary would probably have remained in the wastebasket, where it had been crushed into a ball by an associate editor who called it "The sickest crap I'd run into."

"It was a hell of a long dream, brother, if it didn't happen…"

– Richard Shaver

Blair MacKenzie Blake has been studying, practicing, and writing about the western esoteric tradition for over twenty years. He is the author of two books: *Ijynx* and *The Wickedest Books in the World: Confessions of an Aleister Crowley Bibliophile*. In his 'other life', he is the writer/content manager for www.toolband.com and www.dannycarey.com

WALKING in the SHADOW of DEATH

Exploring the history of 'corpse roads' through archaeology and folklore

by *Lucy Ryder*

A s Benjamin Franklin supposedly said, "The only things certain in life are death and taxes", and with that comes the ceremonial of the final journey. The experience of death, and the procession of the corpse from its home during life to its final abode, held a distinctive and under-investigated role in creating landscapes imbued with symbolism and meaning. The performance and act of moving the body from home to church was intrinsically part of the funeral act, and the consequence of that final passage was that 'Death Roads' became a part of pre-industrial rural landscapes. These so-called Death roads, also known as coffin paths or corpse roads, are found all over Great Britain and Ireland, and are also prevalent in the Netherlands and Germany. However, there has been very little research into their origin, or their place within the organisation and management of the rural landscape, apart from discussion in folkloric or 'new age' literature. This essay will attempt to shed some light on the topic by focusing on what survives archaeologically, and also what occurs in narrative form – through folkloric stories and oral history – and discuss how the presence of death roads affected the way in which the people who lived amongst them saw their surroundings.

So, where do these routes occur? Predominantly (although not exclusively) death roads occur where there are dispersed settlements within the landscape. The term dispersed settlements is a little vague, but traditionally has been described as "solitary building groups or hamlets".[1] Although this is a rather a simplistic view (and whole volumes can, and have, been taken up with debates of what makes a settlement a village and what makes a hamlet), for now this will suit to illustrate the landscape we wish to discuss.

Archaeologically the evidence for death roads is scant, which has naturally led to their relative absence from orthodox study, but in landscape terms a picture can be developed relating to the act of procession, and how this relates to attitudes to the dead in the past. Part of this requires that we address how death was dealt with, and also the values and meaning attached to church/chapel and burial ground, in influencing how the landscape was understood.

DEATH ROADS IN THE LANDSCAPE:
THE RESEARCHER'S VIEW

Although there are some that argue the origins of death roads lie in the prehistoric period, as I will discuss, it is more generally thought that they are the product of Christian 'mother churches' setting distinct rules about burials during the later medieval period. Following the population growth of that period, the large churches

Old Corpse Road in northern England that links Mardale with Swindale and thence to Shap.
(© Michael Graham, licensed under Creative Commons Attribution-Share Alike 2.0)

wanted to keep rural communities tied to them.. As such, funeral rites were forbidden to be given in the communal 'Chapel of Ease' that was situated within each of these growing settlements, – instead, communities would have to take the dead to the main church for the act of burial. This transportation of the dead from hamlets and villages dotted around the countryside created a network of routes across the landscape, often over difficult terrain.

Archaeologically, the significance and the importance of these routes are invisible except for the odd piece of, what Paul Devereux calls "furniture".[2] Frequently the only distinguishing feature of a death road is the occurrence of 'coffin stops', which in reality were frequently just convenient rocks where bearers could rest the coffin or bier along the route.

Conveniently, the routeways that cross the harsh of Cornish terrain of Bodmin leave the most tangible evidence: round headed Celtic crosses line the routes from settlement to church, and acted as way markers and stopping points for the coffin to be rested. These may be been later additions to the route, crosses recycled from other locations or part of their original use, and it is not clear how long they have served to line the way across the moor. But they give us the clearest impression of the scale and extent of the endeavour to take the deceased across the landscape.

Using historic documents as a guide, some of the most tangible evidence for death roads comes from maps attached to the 1535 *Valor Ecclesiasticus* (a survey of church finances ordered by Henry VIII) for the cathedrals of Exeter, Lincoln and Leicester. Named *Barlichway* on the maps, these are routes whose name is derived from a Germanic origin, meaning dead or spirit (in *Notes and Queries from 1860* the editors thought that this was taken from the Saxon words signifying "naked corpse road",[3] but it is more likely to mean just corpse road). The *bar-* prefix to the name is significant, and appears repeatedly in reference to the other, more supernatural creatures that were also supposed to frequent the death roads (more on that later).

As with many elements of landscape history and archaeology, the first significant evidence to the presence of a death or corpse roads are place-names, and these frequently are the only indicator within the landscape of the routes. Field-names, containing these elements are also useful in this context and can record the line of a route where it has been obscured by later farming practices.

Common place/field-name evidence for roadways are:

- bier or burial road
- coffin road, coffin line
- lyke or lych way
- funeral road
- procession way
- corpse way

Once identified, it can be seen that the extent of these routeways is also considerable, and some covered long distances. For example, Lyke

Wake Walk in Osmotherley to the eastern Ravenscar in Yorkshire covered some 40 miles in distance.

However, there was also a common misapprehension that if a funeral procession from one parish crossed the land of another parish with a coffin, that land became the property of the burying parish. This belief seems to have been particularly commonly held in London – Steve Roud, author of *Londone Lore: The Legends and Traditions of the World's Most Vibrant City*, notes that there were numerous occurrences of boroughs stopping a body from passing into their district.[4] This incorrect 'rule' was also frequently used as an explanation for narrow strips of land within one parish being owned by another community. Similarly there was a popular fallacy that "the passage of a corpse over a private road makes that road a public one for ever after",[5] which meant that some of the routes which the death road took was not always the most straightforward, as many landowners forbid the corpses crossing their land.

Interestingly, and perhaps tellingly, many of these routes were used for a number of other innocuous activities which are not memorialised within the landscape or popular consciousness. For example the Corpse Road from Wasdale in Cumbria is one of a number of routes located almost at the water's edge and set apart from a maze of walled-in grassy lanes. This road was also used until the 15th century by the Eskdale community, who travelled the same trackway in the reverse direction to St. Bees – not for burials, but for baptisms. Yet, the naming of the route does not reflect this, and the other roads in the landscape also act as a background buzz of activity to this one singled-out trackway as a road for the dead. What made this activity special? There must have been something of particular significance for the evocative naming and singling out of these routes as death or corpse roads. But again, more on that later...

Looking at the practicalities of the death roads for a little longer, there were many difficulties in getting the dead to the mother churches. Many communities on the Yorkshire moors were forced to store the dead in outbuildings for many months during the winter before transporting them to the Minster Churches. This was particularly so during the mid-17ᵗʰ and 19ᵗʰ centuries, when the region experienced several episodes of extremely harsh winters.

There are some later accounts of the ritualistic nature (by which I mean ceremonial, rather than religious or supernatural at this stage) of the act of carrying the dead across these distances. Turning to a fictional narrative – though clearly drawing on an example from real-life, and undoubtedly recognisable to the reader – is a description of the carrying of the coffin given in *A Son of Hagar* by Sir Hall Cane:

> There were two sets on 'em [Carriers] and they'd a big bottle atween
> '...well they carried Adam shoulder high from the house to the
> grave-yard, first one set and then t'other, mile on mile apiece, and
> when one set got to the end of their mile they set down the coffin
> and went on for t'other set to pick it up. It were nine mile from
> Branthet Edge to Gosforth, so they had nine shifts atween them,
> and at every shift they swigged away at the big bottle...[6]

The idea of teams of bearers was also found on the route of perhaps the most well known corpse road: the Lynch Way from Bellever to Lydford, which covered 12 miles across the hills and valleys of several Tors (Longaford, Lydford and Bagga Tors), before reaching the neatly named Coffin Wood near Lynford. It was here that the body was transferred into a wooden coffin, and specialist pall-bearers took over the carrying of the body to St Pectrocs.

Alongside teams of bearers, another consistency was the ringing of bells when the procession neared it conclusion. In Lake District the church bell was said to ring a certain number of tolls – the "passing toll" – which varied depending on whether the deceased was male or female, or a child.[7]

There is a reference to this practice in the mid-16ᵗʰ century: an extract from parish accounts in 1526 declares "item, the Clarke to have for tollynge of the passynge belle, for manne, womanne, or childes, if it be in the day iiij *d*. Item if it be in the night, for the same viij *d*".[8] It is generally thought that it was one toll for a child, two for a woman, and three for a man. Meanwhile, at Tilston near Chester, bell 1 (of 4) was rung until the corpse was in sight, and then all the bells were chimed until the procession reached the lych gate.[9]

The ringing of the bells in some ways formalised the ritualistic aspect of the procession: before this point in the journey the carrying of the body was a more practical affair – for instance, mourners following the body would sometimes take shortcuts to make the route easier – and less about public displays of solemn grief. But with the announcement of the passing bell, solemn and formal nature of the activity began in earnest.

I do not, however, mean to give the impression that there was no ritual in the procession along the death roads. The procession itself was highly charged with symbolism and structure, and there was an importance to how the group moved across the landscape. Further, there clearly was deep respect held for the designated route of these death roads. Indeed any departure from the route by the corpse and its bearers was taken as an ill omen, even if the mourning followers were cutting corners to avoid floodwaters and boggy land. To emphasise this there is folkloric evidence that funeral parties often faced mortal danger at the crossing of the River Tavy along the Lych Way, as the body and bearers were forced to stick to the prescribed route.

This is where the practical activity of moving the dead to their final resting place meets something less tangible. The act, and more significantly the route, was highly charged with a meaning far beyond the (relatively) simple act of moving from one place to another. This can be clearly seen in an interesting folk belief that was prevalent in North Yorkshire in particular, in which death or corpse roads were seen in some way to 'sterilise' – that is, the dead were forced to walk the route until their soul was purged. Again referring back to the Lych Way, there are stories that a ghostly funeral, led by white monks,

Lych Gate at Strata Florida Abbey in Ceredigion, Wales

can be seen walking the route of the death road around Wistman's Wood, endlessly retracing the route. This puts a completely new layer of complexity onto these routes; this is where practicality is overcome by folklore – these routes are not simply for transporting the dead to their final resting place, rather they have become the tracks set apart for "conveyance with the dead".[10]

FOLKLORE AND PREHISTORIC 'PRETENDERS'

It can clearly be seen then that the function of these routes, to take the dead on their final journey to church and burial, was overlaid with a number of folkloric elements – and as such, their original function is not perfectly clear. It is not a great leap of faith to suggest that the routes represented, to Catholic (and indeed the early protestant) communities, some form of purgatory, and that they are strongly connected to the souls of the dead – we see as much in the writings of Shakespeare. He depicts a commonly held belief in the play *A Midsummer Night's Dream*, one which again shows how death roads were associated with otherworldly journeying. In one scene, Puck states:

> In remembrance of a shroud.
> Now it is the time of night
> That the graves all gaping wide,
> Every one lets forth his sprite,
> In the church-way paths to glide.

The passage suggests that the way to church was not only frequented by the living, but also by the spirits of those interred in the burial grounds – and is heavily reminiscent of the image of the white monks taking their deceased charges across the wilds of Dartmoor mentioned earlier...

The 'Fairy Steps' of Beetham in Cumbria, England (© Raymond Knapman, licensed under
Creative Commons Attribution-Share Alike 2.0)

However, this is where the element of folklore adds an extra layer
of complexity: these 'church-ways', as Shakespeare describes them
were not only the abode of the spirits of the dead. As Katherine
Briggs, author of *The Fairies in Tradition and Literature*, neatly
notes,[11] the dead have also been curiously entangled with fairies in
popular tradition. In doing so, the landscape of death and corpse
roads becomes connected with another layer of myth and tradition;
that is, that they are the places of the *fey*, and that they are 'separate'
spaces from the rest of the landscape.

Indeed, Sir Walter Scott[12,13] noted that death roads (especially in
Devon) were commonly believed to be haunted by monstrous black
dogs. The colloquial name for these beasts, *barguest,* is taken from
the Germanic word *bahrgeist*, meaning spirit of the dead. Here we
see again the occurrence of the *bar-* prefix, linking the dead and the
fey together. Similarly, there is an oral history regarding ghosts or
pixies being sited upon the coffin stones along the route on Haytor

for example, and a number of instances of fairies and pixies using the routes to travel across the landscape.

However, the fascinating folkloric nature of death roads has been, perhaps, its downfall. This is where the real routes and those of, shall we say, 'suspect' origin are mixed together in the more unconventional writings on the subject. Many so-called death or corpse roads discussed in this literature have no real evidence of the original function of moving the dead to the site of their burial, and as such there is some controversy as to what is real and what is merely conjecture.

Prehistoric monuments are frequently associated with death roads, and compared side by side with routes such as the Lych Way, and the Lyke Wake Walk. Stone rows are the most commonly associated – it has been suggested that these rows are spirit roads for the dead ancestors to travel along. Any study of prehistory will show that the role of Neolithic avenues at monuments such as Stonehenge and Avebury clearly had special meaning. The same can be said for the high-banked Neolithic cursuses, such as the one in Dorset that once ran for 10 kilometres across the landscape. This monument clearly demarks one space from another in what appears to be a routeway, but its function remains unknown. With physical evidence of ancient structures such as this, it is perhaps no surprise that stone avenues, such as West Kennet Avenue at Avebury, have been cited as death roads. In the case of West Kennet, this due to the occurrence of the sanctuary and the supposed excarnation that occurred there at one end at the Sanctuary monument, and the henge itself at the other. As we know little of their origin, this might seem a reasonable argument, particularly as an explanation for the configuration of monuments in the landscape.

However, some relationships are less tangible: for example, those associated with stone rows, such as Merrivale on Dartmoor. These monuments have also been labelled as death roads, as it is has been asserted that spirits can only travel in straight lines (explaining, it is argued – somewhat circularly – the shape of the monuments).

Death roads are also frequently associated with ley lines, and are often even described as the same entity. But by taking these monuments out of context – and overlaying 21st century belief structures on to them – we muddy the waters in terms of understanding the relationship between the prehistoric antecedence to the historic death roads we have discussed above. This is where there is discrepancy in the research surrounding death roads, which has perhaps affected the subject's ability to gain academic credence as an area of study.

Death roads may be able to tell us much about not only mortuary practices and landscapes in previous eras, but also give us insights into folk belief and the day to day rituals of the past that have until now been lost to us. However, they must be claimed back from the more speculative studies (which of course have their place) in order to create a more robust understanding of these fascinating networks and their landscapes.

Lucy Ryder is a landscape archaeologist researching landscapes, folklore, perception, and memory. She has a passion for prehistory, but mostly researches the medieval and post medieval period. She is an Honorary Research Associate of the University of Chester and blogs at landscapetales.wordpress.com.

PORTALS ᵒᶠ STRANGENESS

Synchronicity, Symbolism, and Fortean Phenomena.

Or,

What Does It Mean When Weird Things Happen?

by *Ray Grasse*

I was just thirteen at the time, sitting with a friend on the front porch of his home, talking about the sort of things 13-year olds normally talk about, when I noticed an odd light in the distance out of the corner of my eye. He noticed it, too, and we turned our heads to see a glowing disc-shaped object rising up over the trees, probably a half-mile away. It was shaped like the top half of a hamburger bun, I thought, and was cream-colored, with a curious green outline along its fringe. After rising up a short distance, the disc darted around in a strange way, unlike any airplane or hot air balloon I'd seen, before moving off and dropping out of view beneath the tree line. The entire experience lasted maybe 40 seconds in all.

We were stunned by what we'd witnessed, since it was so different from anything else we'd encountered before, outside of Hollywood movies, that is. When we tried describing what we'd witnessed to our parents, our accounts were brushed off as the products of over-active imaginations. I even tried calling up the nearby airport to report what we saw to find out if anyone else mentioned it, but they dismissed my story as simple misidentification. "It was probably just a blimp with advertising lights on it, that's all," he assured me patronizingly. I wasn't sure what we'd seen, and to this day I still don't know; but it's safe to say it wasn't a blimp with advertising lights on it.

We've probably all had brushes at one point or another with something that baffles us, even if that was just an unlikely coincidence or some hunch that turned out to be accurate. But what about the *truly* odd event – like a peculiar craft darting around in the sky? Or a rainfall of frogs from the sky, as a friend's grandmother told me she witnessed as a teenager back in Indiana?

The renegade researcher Charles Fort (1874-1932) spent the better part of his life collecting such stories and compiling them into books like *Lo!* and *The Book of the Damned*, in the process inspiring countless other researchers and even a magazine that commemorates his legacy, *Fortean Times*. Presuming we don't just dismiss all these strange accounts as simple hallucinations, hoaxes, or misidentifications, what are we to make of these tales?

Having studied accounts like these for decades at this point, I'm convinced these events hold profound significance for those experiencing them. In other words, there's something strangely fitting about when and where these events occur, not just for individuals but even for society at large.

What follows is an attempt to provide a framework for understanding these phenomena, through the lens of synchronicity and symbolism. In part, this involves becoming more aware of the larger network of events constellated around these phenomena, since they inevitably seem enmeshed within larger patterns of significance.

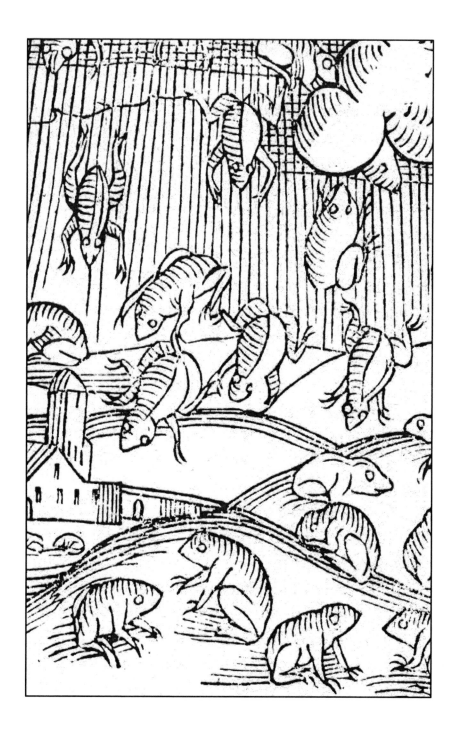

But it also requires the critical step of asking, *What do these events mean?* For as important as these webs of synchronicity are, they mean little if we don't take the time to explore the archetypal meanings involved. Said another way, Fortean phenomena are best understood as elements within an overarching symbolic worldview.

A Synchronistic World View

First, a few definitions of terms would be useful here. The Swiss psychologist Carl Jung defined *synchronicity* simply as "meaningful coincidence," involving the intersection of an outer event with an inner state of mind, or as the correspondence between two outer events. You stumble across a photo of someone you haven't heard from in 20 years, only to have them call you on the phone at that exact moment. That is a simple example of *synchronicity*.

But as I point out in my book *The Waking Dream*, synchronistic phenomena can be understood as fundamentally *symbolic events*. According to various mystical traditions throughout history, our universe can be thought of as an expression of mind-stuff, more akin to our nightly dreams than the "solid" world described by materialists. "Things here are signs," the philosopher Plotinus said.

For that reason outer events can be interpreted in much the same way as dream imagery, concealing layers of symbolism beyond surface appearances. According to this worldview, all phenomena interlock in a profound and intricate way that reflects the workings of a vast intelligence, what the Buddhists refer to as *Big Mind*. Nothing is chance, nothing is disconnected from the whole. In this way, synchronicities – or isolated dramatic coincidences – are actually just the tip of a greater iceberg of meaningfulness that extends throughout our entire lives, and in turn, the cosmos.

But while all phenomena possess a certain significance, one particular kind of event has always been viewed as holding special importance, which I'd summarize this way: *the more unusual an event, the greater its importance as a symbol of change.*

For example, overhearing the same number or name mentioned twice in a single day may be uncommon but it's not particularly unusual. Or seeing a woman in a polka-dot dress may be out of the ordinary but it's nothing shockingly different. But seeing a dog give birth to a two-headed puppy? Now, *that's* unusual! Indeed, the ancient Babylonians made a systematic study of just such oddities as part of their long-term study of omens and symbols, in hope of extracting predictable patterns from their occurrence. The sheer unusualness of such events was taken as signaling tectonic shifts in the natural order.

This is where Fortean events come in, because they're about as unusual as it gets. Strange animals, rainfalls of frogs, time slips, glowing craft flying through the sky, divine apparitions—these rank high on life's Richter Scale of "high strangeness," and hold special significance as signposts of transformation. Those are the types of events I want to focus on here.

That said, I'd like to suggest viewing Fortean events on at least two distinct levels: the personal and collective.

Anomalies: Personal and Collective Significance

For those who experience them, anomalous events invariably happen during times of extraordinary change – emotionally, professionally, intellectually, or spiritually. When I experienced that odd light in the sky, I was undergoing a major change in my own life. Since I kept a diary back then, I was able to go back and see what was happening at the time. Part of that simply involved puberty, of course, but above and beyond that this was a period of explosive new interests for me (this was the 60s, remember!) The appearance of that disc coincided closely with a major shift taking place in my attitudes since I had just started discovering books and articles about subjects beyond just rock and roll, monster movies, or James Bond paperbacks. There was a "meaningful coincidence" between my outer and inner reality then, aptly symbolized by that strange glowing disc. To my mind, it possessed a certain futuristic quality which hinted at progressive new ideas emerging in my own life.

As an astrologer, I've discovered that Fortean events are closely paralleled by important planetary configurations taking shape at the time these phenomena occur. Years after my incident with the glowing disc, for example, I was intrigued to look back and discover that my experience happened precisely as Uranus was forming a powerful relationship to my Mercury—a planetary combination normally associated with surprising or shocking new insights and experiences in one's life. As I'll continue to show here, understanding planetary patterns is often an invaluable key for teasing out subtler inflections from anomalous events.

A HAUNTING

Different anomalous events can hold distinctly different meanings, however. Several years later when I was 15, for example, I had another strange experience while spending the night in a relative's house, an old structure from the 1800s. In the middle of the night, with no external light leaking into the room, I awoke to see a ghostly form at the foot of my bed. It was misty, vaguely human in appearance, and didn't vanish when I rubbed my eyes to clear the sleep from them, as I'd sincerely hoped. When the form didn't go away, I quickly turned over in fright and buried my face deep in my pillow, my heart thumping wildly.

What was it? To this day I don't know. What I *do* know – aside from the fact that it scared me half to death – is that it took place during an extremely emotional time in my life, when I was grappling with an assortment of youthful neurotic issues, particularly regret over a painful social situation I'd encountered several days earlier. (And is there anything more troubling to a teenager than a painful social situation? I think not.)

So in contrast to the unidentified light in the sky several years earlier, which coincided with radical new ideas entering my life, the ghostly encounter seemed to coincide more closely with problems I was struggling to let go of and simply forget. Said another way, the apparent haunting occurred at a time when I was feeling "haunted" myself.

Now, whether that apparition truly *was* a ghost is less important, since my approach here is a more phenomenological one. I *believed* it was a ghost, so within my own experiential matrix at the time it held that basic meaning. In the examples we'll be looking at here I'll be adopting just such a phenomenological approach, rather than trying to judge the reality or illusoriness of the stories being reported. From the symbolist standpoint, there is significance to be mined either way.

Let's turn out attention now to the broader level, and consider what these phenomena could mean for society-at-large.

THE COLLECTIVE SIDE

Just as anomalous events hold a synchronistic meaning for individuals, so they hold significance for the communities or cultures in which they occur, similar to dream symbols but on a much grander scale.

As already mentioned, one way of approaching any anomalous event is by reflecting on its symbolism. In this way, a strange light moving erratically in the sky suggests a different meaning from a ghostly encounter, or for that matter an alleged sea monster, say.

But the other key to understanding an event is by studying its *context*. While our tendency is to see events in relative isolation, Carl Jung and others noted the way ancient cultures like the Chinese employed a kind of "field thinking" which looked at events in groups and asked, *What tends to happen together in time?* Synchronistic thinking requires not only a gift for metaphor and symbolism, but an ability to think holistically, where one perceives the larger patterns constellated around an event.

For example, in June 2013, an ancient Egyptian statuette on display in an English museum was found to have pivoted 180 degrees around on its base. Since they'd never seen that happen with this exhibit before, museum officials were mystified and had no ready explanation. To help solve the mystery, they installed a surveillance camera to observe it over time in hope of finding the source of that movement. Indeed, time-lapse video showed the statuette shifting on its base very slowly over many hours, yet there was still no obvious cause for the shift. Some speculated it was the result of vibrations triggered by passing museum-goers, or a nearby transit train, while still others clung to a more paranormal explanation.

Whatever the reasons, the sheer unusualness of this event invites us to consider its possible symbolism. What does it mean that this story became such a media sensation *right now*? One possibility is to look at the larger historical context around the time it happened, to see if other events might help shed some light on it.

And what we find is this: several weeks later, Egypt underwent a profound transformation as mounting public pressure forced the removal of its Islamic-leaning president, Mohammed Morsi. Could it be that the "about face" of that statue in the Manchester museum was somehow a portent of the political reversal about to upset Egyptian culture itself? For the symbolist, it's an intriguing possibility.[1]

DECODING THE ROSWELL INCIDENT

Another iconic event in the annals of Fortean phenomena was the rumored crash of one or more alien spacecraft near Roswell, New

Mexico in 1947. According to eyewitnesses, the craft was later retrieved by the United States military and reverse-engineered by researchers to procure whatever high-tech secrets it held.

It's important to realize right off that this wasn't the only "otherworldly" phenomenon taking place at the time. Just two weeks earlier, on June 24th, another iconic event in Fortean lore, Kenneth Arnold's sighting of flying discs in Washington State, occurred. And several days before *that*, seaman Harold Dahl claimed to have witnessed six UFOs near Maury Island in Puget Sound, Washington, and the next morning also reported what would be the first documented "Men in Black" encounter.

What does it mean that so many dramatic events centering around UFOs took place in so short a time?

Viewed as a complex of events rather than just as isolated incidents, it's safe to say that the winds of change were in the air. With their hints of advanced intelligences and superior technologies, a futuristic archetype was clearly at work, pointing to emerging new trends in the world.

And indeed, there were a number of historic shifts taking place during this period. Technology was advancing at a breakneck speed,

especially in atomic weaponry and computer development; the CIA
was set into motion that same month; and the United States Air
Force became an independent governmental agency at the same
time. (In fact, a B-25 bomber sent to investigate the Maury Island
incident crashed on August 1st of that year – the very same day the
United States Air Force came into being.) On a global scale, the sense
of optimism that was emerging globally in the wake of WWII was
coupled by a growing sense of anxiety and unpredictability in regions
like China, India, and Israel.

An important key to unlocking what was happening that year
can be found in the astrology of that time. Precisely when all three
of these Fortean incidents took place, the planet Uranus was just
completing its second full circuit around the zodiac from where it was
positioned at its discovery in 1781—a "Uranus return," as astrologers
refer to it. Symbolically, Uranus is the planet of revolution, aviation,
and innovation, so a return to its place of zodiacal origin like this
clearly signals an amplifying of progressive trends and paradigms in
the collective arena.

Because Uranus is the planet associated with the zodiacal sign
Aquarius, it's even possible that the events of that period offer
a significant "window" into the emerging Aquarian Age itself –
which, depending on one's perspective, could be a cause for either
jubilation or lamentation. Were the events of 1947 portending a
future of exciting new technologies, scientific breakthroughs, and
even interaction with extraterrestrial intelligences? Or were those
events warning us about an age of government surveillance, cover-
ups, and technological complications? Or even all of the above? One
way or another, it will be interesting to watch the next major return
of Uranus to that discovery point – slated to take place in 2030-2031.

Let's turn our attention now to one of the most iconic events in all
of Fortean folklore — the filming of an alleged Bigfoot in California
by Roger Patterson and Bob Gimlin on October 20th of 1967.

The Patterson-Gimlin "Bigfoot" Film

As the story goes, Roger and Bob were traveling on horseback through an area called Bluff Creek, when they spotted a large dark figure in a nearby creek bed. Patterson climbed down off his horse, grabbed the movie camera he had with him at the time, and proceeded to film the creature as it lumbered off into the woods.

To this day, the footage remains a source of heated debate, yet despite repeated claims by skeptics of possible hoaxing it's important to point out no one has ever successfully reproduced the appearance of that creature on film in a remotely convincing way. Whatever one's opinion about the film, all parties agree that the footage represents a turning point in our modern fascination with this creature, and for that reason it represents a synchro-Fortean event of the highest order.

Taking a purely symbolic approach to the footage, we could start by looking at it strictly in terms of its imagery, as if examining someone's dream symbolism. The creature in this footage is obviously wild and untamed, halfway between human and animal, straddling the threshold between civilization and nature. It's entirely naked and covered with fur, yet it stands upright and walks similar to how a human does. Its muscular figure conveys a sense of enormous power, yet at the same time it displays female breasts!

Viewed as a collective dream symbol, then, the appearance of this creature in 1967 can be read as signaling something primal surfacing from the "wilds" of the collective unconscious, an energy paradoxically ancient yet new and shocking. The figure embodies great power, yet its feminine gender hints at a consciousness that is more right-brain and intuitive than anything purely aggressive or animalistic. It personifies a condition of being midway between ordered civilization and untamed nature, betwixt pure rationality and raw emotional impulses.

With those points in mind, let's now adopt our Chinese "field thinking" approach and see what other socio-cultural developments were taking place around that encounter, to see if anything stands out which might illumine the symbolism suggested here. When I went back and carefully examined the historical record from that period, I came across a number of events that seemed not only relevant, but at times truly uncanny:

- Two days before the Patterson-Gimlin encounter, on October 18, Disney Studios released the popular animated feature *The Jungle Book*. The film's scenario revolves around a boy raised by animals in the wild, and follows his escapades as he mingles on the threshold between nature and civilization, between life in the wild and domesticated village life.

- One day before that, on October 17th, the enormously successful musical *Hair* premiered on Broadway. This long-running production was embraced by fans as a celebration of freedom and Dionysian self-expression, but was slammed by some conservative critics as regressively promoting amorality and primitive values. The musical's title itself hints at how the hippies at its core shunned the neatly groomed fashions of mainstream society in favor of wilder, more natural looks. The musical became especially controversial for a scene in which all the cast members appeared on stage fully naked.

- Less than a week earlier, on October 12th, Desmond Morris's bestselling book *The Naked Ape* was released, a popularized attempt to frame human nature in the context of Darwinian evolution. It suggested that we need to view humans as just one animal species among many, and tried to explain our behaviors in light of those exhibited by our mammalian kin. The book was so titled because out of 193 species of money and apes, humans are the only ones not fully covered in hair.

- Three weeks after the Patterson-Gimlin encounter, the Bible of the rock-and roll counterculture, *Rolling Stone*, premiered. (November 9th was the cover date on the first issue, but as is common practice in the publishing industry, it appeared on newsstands earlier.) Contrasted with publications like the ultra-conservative Wall Street Journal, with that paper's embrace of short haircuts, business suits, and "square" values, Rolling Stone celebrated much the same ideas as the musical "Hair"—alternate lifestyles, long hair, music, and Dionysian self-expression. Though it spawned many imitators through the years, it remains an influential magazine to this day.

- The human/primate interface was a surprisingly popular meme in all the arts throughout this period. Several months after the P-G incident, on February 8th, 1968, the first in the hugely successful *Planet of the Apes* film franchise premiered, centering around a society of unusually intelligent apes; while 1967 saw the peak popularity of the TV show *The Monkees*, showcasing a group of long-haired Beatle imitators (and whose records actually outsold both the Beatles and the Rolling Stones that year), with episodes frequently picturing the actors alongside images of actual or stuffed monkeys.

- Another way that the counter-cultural impulses of the period were making their presence felt was through the burgeoning protest movement, with ordinary citizens rallying to express their anger over governmental policies—a development some commentators described as "the awakening of a sleeping giant." In light of that, it's worth noting that one day after the Patterson-Gimlin encounter a historic march on Washington, D.C. took place, as tens of thousands of citizens lined the streets of the nation's capital to protest America's involvement in the Vietnam War.[2] As clearly as any other event from that period, this march embodied the grassroots energies of the 60's surfacing in a dramatic way.

Putting all of these pieces together, the picture that starts to emerge is indeed that of a powerful force welling up in the collective psyche—a force simultaneously rooted in the intuitive-emotional aspects of our nature as well as our more rational faculties. (After all, developments like *Hair, The Jungle Book, Rolling Stone,* and the march on Washington weren't just expressions of Dioynysian abandon and unbridled anarchy, since their execution all involved considerable planning and intelligence.)

Simply consider the 1960's, and all the countercultural forces that were coming to light at the time: people were shedding their conservative fashions and adopting wilder, more uninhibited appearances. The Back-To-Nature movement was on the rise, with 1967 ushering in the "Summer of Love" and "Flower Power." The Beatles released "Sergeant Pepper" that year. There was a general sense of heightened creativity in the air, as people from various walks of life woke up to the possibility of becoming forces for change in the world, whether as grass-roots activists or celebrities and rock stars.

Yet alongside all this was a palpable sense of danger and potential violence, as all those pent-up energies found themselves being unleashed, which was reflected not just in protest movements, big city riots, or bombings, but even in the arts. One month before the Patterson-Gimlin encounter, for instance, on September 17th,

The Doors courted controversy by appearing on the Ed Sullivan show with Jim Morrison singing a drug-related lyric in defiance of the host's wishes, while that same night The Who destroyed their instruments while performing on The Smothers Brothers Comedy Hour, climaxing in an unexpectedly jarring explosion of Keith Moon's drum kit. Several months earlier, a relative unknown named Jimi Hendrix shocked audience members at the Monterey Pop Festival in California by dry-humping his amplifier and setting fire to his prized guitar. Wild times, indeed.

Seen in this context, the first major film appearance of an alleged Bigfoot seems like an apt symbol for the entire period. Midway between human and animal, this creature mirrored a powerful instinctual energy surging forth in the collective psyche, yet one coupled with a newly awakened sense of individuality and independent thought. Remember, this wasn't simply a beast, but an apparently intelligent one that walked upright like ourselves. Similarly, people of that time were trying to juggle starkly polarized energies in themselves, born from that divide between our loftiest creative impulses and our most primal passions.

Astrologically, the Patterson-Gimlin encounter took place during a powerful astrological alignment between the planets Uranus and Pluto—a celestial duo typically associated with revolutionary change and volatile emotions, such as occurred in France during the 1790's. As I write this now (2013), the world finds itself in the midst of the next major configuration involving these planets to occur since the 1960's, as they reconnect now in a 90-degree angle. Not surprisingly, we not only see signs of civil unrest in countries around the world but, curiously enough, the phenomenon of Bigfoot has reached an all-time high, with TV series, books, and pop culture references to the creature popping up seemingly everywhere. Is it possible we could even see another milestone in the Bigfoot story unfolding soon? Time will tell.

THE LOCH NESS MONSTER

The Patterson-Gimlin incident provides a useful springboard for considering another mainstay of Fortean lore—Scotland's legendary Loch Ness Monster. While sightings of the creature actually date back centuries, modern fascination with this phenomenon began in 1933—specifically May 2nd, when journalist Alex Campbell first applied the term "monster" in an article he wrote for the *Inverness Courier*.

As it turned out, 1933 was a pivotal year in a number of key respects. For instance, less than six weeks before Campbell's article was published, Adolph Hitler became formally established as dictator of Germany, on March 23rd. And just three weeks before that, on March 2nd, the world was introduced to a Fortean creature of a fictional sort, with the film premiere of *King Kong*.

With that in mind, the "coming out" of the Loch Ness creature in 1933 offers a surreal metaphor for the spirit of that era. Like the mid-1960's, this was a time of powerful emotional energies rising to the surface, in both constructive and destructive ways. The advent of Hitler and the premiere of *King Kong* during the same month

synchronistically parallel one another, since both represented figures of immense power that grew out of control and terrorized civilized society, then were ultimately destroyed themselves. In the midst of this, the Scottish leviathan surfacing into public consciousness can be seen as a portent for the turbulent times that loomed ahead. (Interestingly, 1933 was also accompanied by a tight configuration between those two powerhouse planets Uranus and Pluto, similar to what occurred when that other oversized primate made its screen debut for Roger Patterson and Bob Gimlin in 1967.)

ONE STEP BEYOND

I've suggested here at least two different levels of importance to Fortean events, the personal and the collective, but I'd like to touch briefly on another possible level of significance: the universal. What does that mean, exactly? Simply, that Fortean events of the most dramatic kind may be saying something important, perhaps even revolutionary, about the nature of the universe itself. Let me explain.

In some instances, an unusual event may simply be that—an unusual event, something out of the ordinary but nothing fundamentally radical. For thousands of years people saw rocks falling from the sky, with these reports being dismissed as nonsensical even by such distinguished thinkers as Thomas Jefferson. Yet scientists eventually discovered those falling rocks were very natural, and labeled them "meteorites." They weren't anything paranormal or truly mysterious, just unknown up to that point. Likewise, reports of the Mountain Gorilla were considered anecdotal and anomalous until proof for their existence finally came to light in 1902 (during yet another configuration involving Uranus and Pluto, by the way!). As a result, things that at one time would have been considered "Fortean" wouldn't be now, unless they involved extremely unusual circumstances.

But then there are Fortean events of a very different order, phenomena of such inherent mystery and high strangeness they seemingly fly in the face of all science and logic. In this category we might include stories of "time slips" where events or individuals from other eras intersect with present-day situations; rainfalls of frogs or fish from the sky; sightings of angelic or mythical beings; or bizarre animals so fantastic they stretch credulity to the breaking point.

One example of this last category would be stories of Mothman, a large humanoid creature with glowing red eyes and wings reportedly sighted in West Virginia during the 1960's and that's been glimpsed on occasion in other regions as well. The fact that a man-size creature with wings could even become airborne seems patently absurd on its surface, yet scores of witnesses swear to what they saw, and their stories coincide in intriguing ways. It's worth noting that the bulk of these sightings preceded a major tragedy in December of 1967, when the Silver Bridge collapsed into West Virginia's Ohio River, killing 46 people; notably, though, sightings of the Mothman in that area ceased after the tragedy, inviting speculations whether the creature's appearance may have been an omen for the impending disaster somehow.

While I can't speak to the objective truth of bizarre sightings like this, I confess that I'm not as inclined to dismiss them out of hand after having had an encounter with a mystery animal once myself, and which remains unexplained to me even today.

I was 29 years old at the time, and visiting a former teacher of mine from Chicago, Maureen, at her new home in Colorado where she lived with her two young girls. The four of us decided to take a drive up through the nearby mountains one afternoon, following a narrow road that carried us up progressively higher, when at one point we all noticed a large black dog cross from one side of the road to the other, roughly 70 or 80 feet in front of our car. Nothing unusual in that, on the surface of things anyway (other than the presence of a dog in such a remote location). But on reaching the other side of the road, the dog simply disappeared into the side of the mountain. Maura, myself, and her children all looked at one another in puzzlement, because it seemed as if the dog had vanished into thin air—or solid rock, as the case may be.

There was no real vegetation or brush in that spot, so my first sense was it must have crawled into a hidden crevasse or gully we simply couldn't see from our current vantage point. But as we slowly drove past where the animal disappeared, it became obvious there was no place it could have gone, since there was no crevasse or gully there, just solid rock. Just to make sure, though, we stopped the car and got out to look around, but that only deepened the mystery. I knew what I had seen, and Maura was an intelligent observer herself, having taught psychology during her academic days at the University of Chicago; and her two children saw the dog, too, making four witnesses to the event in all.

What was it? I still don't have any good explanation for it. On a personal level, I detect a certain symbolic meaningfulness in it, since it happened at a turning point in my life when I was undergoing major emotional changes and self-reflection with my 30th birthday fast approaching. As one possibility, the image of "crossing a road" could be interpreted as a transitional symbol, similar to the crossing of a river or a country's borders. In fact, just one week earlier I'd hiked into the Grand Canyon and experienced a personal epiphany of sorts while crossing a footbridge suspended over the Colorado River at Canyon's bottom. Historically, too, there is a considerably body of folklore involving apparitions or sightings of large black dogs. So there are several possible ways of interpreting the event.

But apart from its possible meaning for each of as individuals, I've often wondered a great deal about what an event like this means in terms of *reality itself.* Perhaps what Fortean phenomena of high strangeness like this say is that we don't know nearly as much about the universe as we thought. Our conventional world may overlap with other dimensions and vibrational realms similar to the way radio and television waves surround us now, though we may be unaware of them.

Fortean events could represent tears in the fabric of reality which allow other dimensions to bleed through into ours, reflecting a true cross-pollination of dimensions. Such experiences seem to occur during times that feel special or are filled with numinosity, what the Greeks described as *kairos*, or sacred time. They often possess an archetypal resonance, allowing us to expand the boundaries of our consciousness and catch momentary glimpses of the larger ocean of possibilities we swim within. In the end, Fortean events may represent portals into a different way of understanding our universe, and ultimately, ourselves.

Ray Grasse is the author of *The Waking Dream: Unlocking the Symbolic Language of Our Lives* (Quest Books, 1996) and *Signs of the Times: Unlocking the Symbolic Language of World Events* (Hampton Roads, 2002). He worked on the editorial staffs of *The Quest Magazine* and Quest Books for ten years, and has studied extensively with teachers in both the Kriya Yoga and Zen traditions. His website is www.raygrasse.com.

Gunung Padang Megalith Site, West Java, Indonesia. (Mohammad Fadli, Creative Commons)

THE Ancient
MOUNTAIN OF LIGHT

HAVE RESEARCHERS FOUND A 24,000-YEAR-OLD PYRAMID IN INDONESIA?

by *Martin J. Clemens*

In the science world, much of the research is inaccessible to the layman. If the concepts being studied aren't orders of magnitude over the heads of the general public, then the means to participate are just not available, whether due to cost or physical location. There are exceptions, however, such as astronomy. In fact, amateur astronomers have been integral to progress in the field, and professional scientists welcome their input, often using their backyard observations as a starting point in the process of discovering some of the most interesting objects and events in the night sky.

Archaeology is sometimes thought of in those same terms, though that really depends on who you ask. Archaeology is the study of human activity in the past, through observation and analysis of the effects of material culture. Essentially, that means that archaeologists look at artefacts and locations and try to determine what those items mean within the context of the particular culture in question. It can be a difficult process, and it requires those who undertake it to be well-read in the humanities, and to have a background in the physical sciences. They must be experts on history, and be conversant in psychology, biology and sometimes physics. But these things aren't exclusive to archaeologists. Anyone can be well-read on the humanities. Many laymen are experts on history and are conversant in biology and physics. And since almost every archaeological find is ultimately dependent on subjective interpretation, it would seem that the field is more open than some would like to think.

The products of archaeology are not the artefacts and ancient buildings that they study; the product is the information gleaned from those items. The dusty trinkets and buried structures are the tools archaeologists use to measure the impact lost cultures had on their environment, and on the members of their societies. The problem arises when that story, or stories as the case may be, don't readily betray the secrets of their originators. Even among the so-called experts, agreement is hard to come by, and when those who look in on the golden circle from the outside get into the fray, things can get messy.

In the world of archaeology, there are some basic truths that form the foundation of the study. One of those truths is the general anthropological timeline, which outlines not only the progression of human development, from the early emergence out of Africa, to our spread throughout Asia and Europe and eventually Australia and the Americas. Other foundational elements include the individual demographics and histories of all of the various civilizations that existed between then and now. But that timeline is only a truth in so far as the majority believe it to be...and there are other voices in the crowd.

It has generally been thought that our ancestors began building monuments and structures for ritual purposes at a specific time in our history. That time is roughly 9000 years ago, or in the 7th millennium BCE. The prevailing wisdom of archaeology says that disparate cultures across Europe and Asia began developing the skills necessary to construct long lasting works of art and primitive architecture using stone as a medium around this time. There were probably many failed starts and half-developed projects that never saw the light of day, but of the examples we know about, the oldest are apparently no older than about 7000 years, indicating that it took roughly 2000 years to hone our skills. By about 5000 years ago, we were building sophisticated structures like Stonehenge in Wiltshire, England, and thus our progression from primitive hunter-gatherer societies to agrarian societies with the time and wherewithal to develop a culture of our own was well underway.

One important aspect of the above, is the implied idea that these skills were developed independently by different cultures. Each culture, we're told, invented, practised and perfected their techniques on their own, with little to no help from other peoples. This is the accepted wisdom.

There are elements of the archaeological record that would seem to disagree however. One of those elements is a megalithic/Neolithic site in the Southeast Anatolia region of modern-day Turkey: Göbekli Tepe.

BREAKING ORTHODOX HISTORY

Discovered in 1964 through an archaeological survey conducted by researchers from Istanbul University and the University of Chicago, Göbekli Tepe is a temple structure consisting of several T-shaped stone pillars and round structures. The pillars are decorated with stylized, anthropomorphic carvings of animals and crude humanoids, and in general the site fits with the standard archaeological timeline

Animal carving on T-shaped pillar at Göbekli Tepe

in terms of its construction and artwork. However, when researchers dated the site they found something quite incredible. It was built in the 10th millennium BCE.

That's at least 4000 years earlier than any other structure of similar sophistication and construction anywhere in the world. This discovery alone is exciting for its implications, and its potential to alter the accepted timeline – and there are those in the old guard of archaeology who refuse to accept that age, for the very reason that it challenges the accepted wisdom.

There are several methods of dating ancient material and artefacts. Visual inspection and comparison to similar artefacts of known age is the very bottom of that scale, and radiometric dating is at the top. The various clocks we use in this process are all based on measuring the decay rates of certain naturally occurring radioactive elements contained within all organic material. These elements, carbon-14 being one of the many available, have defined and universally consistent half-lives – meaning that over a given period of time, the isotope will decay at a certain speed – and when we compare the amount of that element contained within the artefact being dated to these half-life measurements, we come away with a general but solid understanding of the age of that item.

There are problems with this process, however. Firstly, of the various isotopes that can be measured, all of them have half-lives between thousands of years to millions and even billions of years. This is why we use so many different elements as clocks in the dating process, and it means that for any given analysis, we can only get a date-*range* for an artefact. Beyond a certain age, we cannot say that an artefact or structure is "x number of years old"; we can only say that it's "at least as old as", or that it "dates to between x age and y age". And of course, the larger the clock scale, the greater the margin of error. When your reference isotope decays over a period of millions of years, you aren't going to be able to pinpoint an age to within a thousand years.

The second problem is that not all materials can be dated radiometrically. Stone or rock cannot be dated directly. The age of a rock can only be determined by its relationship to other materials that can be dated. In geology, the terms *superposition, faunal succession, crosscutting relationships* and *inclusions* relate to the methods used for determining the age of a rock, and they all refer to material that is found with or inside the rock in question. What this means is that, in a site such as Göbekli Tepe, the age of the site can only be found by dating organic material found underneath or within the stone used to build it. The idea being that such material is going to be related to the age of the structure, because it was in place prior to the structure being built or the stone being placed in position. This presents a unique problem. It means that the dates given for sites such as Göbekli Tepe are not really of the site. They are indirect conclusions extended to the site by logical inference. If, by some weird coincidence, organic material that is older or younger than the site managed to contaminate the samples used in the radiometric dating, the results would be skewed and inaccurate.

Göbekli Tepe excavation, Turkey (Teomancimit, Creative Commons)

This inherent uncertainty in the process is both a blessing and a curse. It is used by archaeologists to both include certain sites in specific cultural epochs and to exclude them, and as may seem convenient, several such people reject the given age of Göbekli Tepe on these grounds.

But another Neolithic site also has the potential to shatter the accepted wisdom of our history, and to bring about a new paradigm of understanding with regard to ancient culture and development. That site is Gunung Padang in Indonesia.

THE MOUNTAIN OF LIGHT

Gunung Padang is a series of stone-walled terraces and standing-stone shapes that sit atop Mount Padang, in or near the village of Karyamukti in the Cianjur regency of West Java, Indonesia. Though it has been known to locals for millennia, it was first described academically in the Dutch naturalist manual *Rapporten van de Oudheidkundige Dienst* in 1914. Not much had been known about it outside of that brief mention until recently, and now it's embroiled in ongoing controversy.

Several teams of geologists and archaeologists have given Gunung Padang serious attention, and initial dates for the site were given as between 500 and 1500 BCE, and then eventually to 5000 BCE. That date puts it in line with other Neolithic sites in Europe, such as Stonehenge, and isn't entirely unexpected, as the parent cultures in both regions are thought to be about the same age.

The site is used, even today, by the Sundanese people of West Java as a place of reflection, meditation and spiritual energy, and the entire hill is considered sacred to their culture. The name means "Mountain of Light" or "Mountain of Enlightenment" in the local Sundanese dialect. This reverence for the site has hampered efforts to study its origins and significance, and though its surface has been fully surveyed, little was known about what lies underneath it.

That all changed in 2012 with geologic testing undertaken by the government of Indonesia. Researchers used ground-penetrating radar (tomography) and geoelectric analysis to determine what the visible site is built on. They found that Mount Padang is not just a hill; instead, they believe it is actually a pyramid. Researchers claimed to have imaged structures, courtyards, pillars, and buried terraces, all indicating that the structure was built in the manner of a stepped pyramid.

This finding is astounding all on its own. Asia has relatively few pyramids, in any style, and some have long wondered why that should be, when other cultures of the same age and younger were prolific in the building of pyramid-type structures. As such, it has been asked, rhetorically, if there are more pyramids in Asia than are apparent; are these ancient structures just hidden from view beneath natural overgrowth?

Just in terms of our collective understanding of Asia's early cultural development, the discovery of the Gunung Padang pyramid is extremely important, but there's much more to it than that.

Armed with this new information, researchers redirected their attention away from investigating what could be seen on the surface, and focused their efforts underground. They undertook a geological survey that included drilling several core samples at various locations around the site. Core sampling, in case you are unfamiliar, is the process of using specialised equipment to obtain a cylindrical shaft of material from whatever is beneath the drilling site, ultimately giving a cross-section of that material going down several meters. From that, analysts can determine the true tomography of the site, by understanding how each layer of material was formed or constructed, and incidentally, date such material. And this is where things get a little weird.

According to some, namely Dr. Daniel Natawidjaja, senior geologist of the Research Center for Geotechnology at the Indonesian Institute of Science (an organization operated by the Indonesian government), the core samples confirmed the earlier findings that suggested that the hill was indeed manmade. Natawidjaja explains that the core samples provided evidence of complex structures and pillars, and most interestingly a material thought to be an early form of mortar cement. It's speculated that this cement, which is found to consist of 45% iron ore, 41% silica, and 14% clay, was used as a mortar base to strengthen rock pile walls and pillars, and to repair elements of the structure that suffered damage over the years.

As the material was analysed and dated, using the radiometric dating techniques described above, researchers began to get very excited. As they drilled deeper and deeper into the hill (or pyramid), they found that the material was older and older. They produced dates from 3000BCE to 5000BCE, to 10,000BCE, and at 90 feet below the surface, they found material that is approximately 24,000 years old, putting the origin of this site at 22,000 BCE.

Needless to say, such dating holds the potential to shatter the accepted wisdom regarding our history. If they hold up, it would place the culture responsible for building Gunung Padang squarely in the peak of the last ice age, a time when conventional wisdom says humanity's numbers were at the lowest they've ever been. According to history text books, it shouldn't have been possible that an ancient civilization existed which was capable of this level of development and architectural sophistication, but there it is.

An Alternative History?

Enter the alternative history theorists. There is a certain movement in fringe culture, a community of sorts, of individuals who study these kinds of findings and use them to challenge the status quo, as it were. And some from this community now assert that these sites, Göbekli Tepe and Gunung Padang, could be direct evidence of an advanced prehistoric culture that has been left out of the history books.

Some, such as author Graham Hancock, theorise that Gunung Padang is evidence of the Lost City of Atlantis. Atlantis, of course, is the famed super-culture described by the ancient Greek philosopher Plato, in his famed Socratic dialogues titled *Critias* and *Timaeus*. Atlantis has been the focus of a great many alternative history theories, and is the obsession of many academics and historians. Supposed evidence of it has been found all over the world, though none, thus far, has really panned out. There are reasonable criticisms of the idea that Gunung Padang has anything to do with Atlantis, even just by virtue of its location. It is so far removed from the historical origins of the story that it's almost laughable, but the timeline seems right.

Others, namely senior advisor to the Indonesian President, Andi Arief, suggest that Gunung Padang is actually a remnant of the lost civilization of Mu.

You may not be familiar with the people of Mu, but their legend is almost as wild as that of Atlantis. Mu is a supposed *lost continent*, and was first hypothesised by 19th century author Augustus Le Plongeon. Le Plongeon was a historian specialising in Mayan culture, and he wrote extensively on the subject. He was the primary proponent of the theory that the Mayans predated the Egyptians, and he believed that all of the major ancient cultures were first populated by refugees from the lost or sunken continent of Mu, which he theorised to have once been a landmass in the Atlantic Ocean.

Le Plongeon's theory was later taken up by author and inventor James Churchward, who claimed to have found ancient stone tablets from the lost people of Mu, who were known as the Naacals. Through his research, Churchward placed Mu in the Pacific Ocean, connecting the Hawaiian Islands with Easter Island and the Polynesian Archipelago.

Both Le Plongeon and Churchward believed that the Naacals of Mu were the parent culture for the early civilizations of India, Babylon, Persia, Egypt and the Maya. Mu's given proximity to Southeast Asia

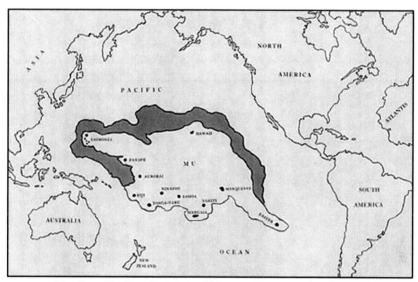

Map from *The Lost Continent of Mu*, 1927. By james Churchward.

and Gunung Padang might have provided opportunity for travel between those two areas during the suggested timeline.

Whether we're talking about Atlantis or Mu, or Lemuria even, the results of the study at Gunung Padang do seem to point to the existence of some kind of advanced culture that apparently flourished during the last ice age. But critics are quite vocal in their opposition to this idea.

As far as the radiometric dating of Gunung Padang is concerned, everything is on the up and up. The analysis was done by a reputable, and some would say, prestigious lab in the US (BETALABS), so the numbers are considered solid. The material they dug up is without a doubt roughly 24,000 years old. But what did they dig up?

The entire story rests on a single point, a point that most in mainstream archaeology deny is valid. Is Gunung Padang a pyramid or similar structure, or is it just a hill? While the tomography results do seem to suggest that there is some kind of structure beneath the visible monument, the conclusion may be premature. All of the work done to date has been undertaken by professional geologists, whose normal purview is rocks and the environment, not archaeological material. This doesn't necessarily invalidate their work – after all, they use the same techniques in their work as archaeologists do – but it does leave open a door for criticism.

If the underground 'structure' beneath the ruins of Gunung Padang was not in fact man-made, then it follows that the material that was dated wasn't associated with a specific artefact or structure. It was just organic material that was pulled out of the ground based on the preliminary tomography results. If the hill that the ruins of Gunung Padang sit upon is just a natural formation, the mystery of the anomalous dating instantly disappears. Indeed, it is thought by most who oppose the theory that the hill is actually a volcanic cone or mound, which would mean that the material used in the radiometric dating was just volcanic dirt, and it wouldn't be surprising to find that such material is quite old.

One other concerning feature of the story is that the Indonesian government has – and has long had – a penchant for politically twisting the history of its country in an effort to compete with its neighbour, China. It seems that some Indonesian leaders want to establish their country as the birthplace of Asian culture, and they tend to seek out storylines that confirm that bias. Andi Arief, the senior advisor to the Indonesian President mentioned above, is a well-known proponent of the One World Origin theory, which claims that all of the major civilizations in our history were parented by a single large and highly developed civilization that has since been lost to time. So it's not surprising to find that he has been instrumental in disseminating the theory that Gunung Padang is evidence of such.

In the end, we have an interesting story, but still not a lot of real information to go on. Does Göbekli Tepe indicate that humanity developed sophisticated architectural techniques before it is generally accepted to have emerged? Is Gunung Padang evidence of a lost civilization, one that may have been part of an unknown One World Origin?

The jury is still out, but there are seemingly good arguments from both sides, and so the research continues.

Martin J. Clemens is a Fortean blogger, and a former investigator and researcher from Ontario, Canada. He blogs at www.paranormalpeopleonline.com and www.mysteriousuniverse.com

Life, Death,
and *Raymond*

Exploring the nature of death
and consciousness

by *Robert M. Schoch, Ph.D.*

Some people are obsessed with death and the question of whether there is a life beyond the life we know in this mortal world of the physical-material plane. Needless to say, many of the great religions, as well as disparate spiritual beliefs around the world, hold that there is something more, something in addition to, the life we experience for a short duration on planet Earth. These ideas are intimately related to the questions: What is mind? What is thought? What is consciousness? Are mind, thought, and consciousness simply electrochemical manifestations of the conglomeration of our nervous tissue, or are they something more, something independent of our current material form?

Sir Oliver Lodge and the Death of Raymond

Today, for the most part, conventional status quo scientists spurn questions about life after death. In fact, not only do they ignore such issues, but also many actively deride anyone who should attempt to address them. There are those who are proud to be staunch atheists determined to spread the word that life on this planet is nothing more than what you see in the physical realm. Death is the end of all, and ultimately life is all rather pointless and meaningless according to such persons.

This has not always been the case. In the late nineteenth and early twentieth centuries such questions were taken up, and taken seriously, by various prominent scientists of the time, including the British physicist Sir Oliver Joseph Lodge (1851-1940). Lodge received a Doctorate of Science from the University of London in 1877 and pursued original and important research in electricity, electromagnetism, and early wireless radio technology throughout his life. He was also a well-established academic in that he was a professor of physics and mathematics at University College, Liverpool, and first Principal (the chief executive and academic officer) of Birmingham University from 1900 until his retirement in 1919. Among the many honors Lodge received for his scientific contributions were the Rumford Medal of the Royal Society of London and knighthood (thus giving him the title of Sir) from King Edward VII in 1902.

Besides his more conventional studies, Lodge was extremely interested in what at the time were generally referred to as psychical studies, and today might be referred to as paranormal manifestations, such as ostensible ghosts, telepathy (direct mind-to-mind communication), and the possibility of life after death. Beginning as early as the 1880s Lodge was involved in séances and experiments regarding such phenomena, he became a member of the Society for Psychical Research (even taking his turn to serve as its president), and he was closely associated with the Spiritualist movement of the

Sir Oliver Lodge

Raymond Lodge

time. Based on both experimental and anecdotal evidence, Lodge was convinced that telepathy is real (looking at the data, much of which has been developed since Lodge's time, I agree with this assessment[1]). Building on his work as a physicist, Lodge variously postulated that telepathy might have something to do with a form of otherwise unknown radiations, possibly of an electromagnetic nature. He also became convinced that there is life after death (publishing a book on the subject in 1909)[2] consisting of a "spirit world" that can at times interact and communicate with our world. This spirit world might exist in the "ether" that Lodge believed pervaded the Universe.

The First World War (1914-1918) brought a tragic loss for Sir Oliver Lodge, but also served as reaffirmation of his belief in an afterlife. Lodge and his wife Lady Lodge (Mary Fanny Alexander Marshall) had twelve children born between 1878 and 1896 in addition to several children who were either stillbirths or died shortly after birth. In September 1914 his youngest son, Raymond (born 1889), volunteered for military service with the British army. After training, Raymond was sent to the European Western Front in the spring of 1915 with the rank of Second Lieutenant. A shell fragment hit him during an attack on Hooge Hill (near Ypres), Flanders, Belgium, on the morning of 14 September 1915 and he died about noon. Sir Oliver Lodge and his family did not learn of Raymond's death until three days later, on 17 September 1915.[3]

SPIRIT COMMUNICATIONS

During the following months Lodge and various members of his family became convinced that they were able to communicate with the now deceased Raymond, particularly during séances orchestrated through established mediums (persons who apparently have the ability to communicate with the "other side"). Sir Oliver Lodge became more convinced than ever that there is a genuine "life after death" and he published a book on the subject, focused on the messages from Raymond.[4] The first edition came out in November 1916 as the war still raged. Arguably the evidence of *Raymond* is among the best direct evidence for the reality of an afterlife.

The spirit communications regarding Raymond may have begun even before his tragic death. In early August 1915 a somewhat ambivalent message was received during a séance, by way of a classical allusion to a passage from the Roman poet Horace (65-8 BCE), that some tragedy would befall Sir Oliver Lodge. However, Lodge's former friend, classics scholar, and fellow psychical researcher Frederic W. H. Myers (1843-1901), who now existed only in the spirit world, promised to help Lodge through the difficult period. Raymond, once he had passed to the other world, communicated that Myers befriended him.

Raymond died on 14 September and the family did not learn of his death until 17 September, yet Sir Oliver Lodge found himself in a terrible state of depression on the 15th, so much so that he was not able to finish a game of golf in Scotland, specially arranged long before, that he had very much been looking forward to. "Sensing" Raymond's death by paranormal means may well have brought on the depression, he felt. Likewise, Raymond's brother Alec (1881-1938) – who had been especially close to Raymond – had a vivid and painful nightmare (although he did not remember that it was about Raymond or anyone in particular) the night of 16/17 September just prior to the morning he received a telegram relating the death of Raymond.

The first communications from Raymond, now on the other side, came in September 1915 shortly after his death. Like many – indeed most – supposed communications from the "spirit world", the majority of communications were unverifiable and non-evidential. That is, there was no realistic way to demonstrate that they were genuinely coming from "Raymond" (or anyone else, for that matter) on the "other side" versus coming from the imagination or subconscious of the medium, those sitting at the séance, or even from other living persons via telepathic connection. If you think about it, many communications that are not face-to-face in the modern era, such as emails, are equally unverifiable and non-evidential in terms of the sender – that is, how do you know an email was really sent by a certain person versus someone posing as that person? Some of the unverifiable and non-evidential communications from "Raymond" seemed, even in Sir Oliver Lodge's initial opinion, to be on their face rather ridiculous and absurd, such as reports of smoking cigars in the afterlife – but then do we really know how to judge such communications?

It is evidential cases of communication, when the communicator – in this case "Raymond" – provides information that helps to verify or prove that he or she really is the person who claims to be on the "other side", that are the most important in attempting to establish the reality of an afterlife. Sir Oliver Lodge recorded several instances, which he regarded as being evidential. For example, Raymond discussed family outings at Woolacombe Beach (North Devon, England), which included a description of a canvas tent on wheels that Raymond and his brothers had constructed and subsequently reconstructed after it was damaged during a gale. The spirit form of Raymond also discussed a sand-boat (a sailboat-like

Alec Lodge seated in the sand-boat at Woolacombe Beach (North Devon, England), 1906
(from *Raymond, or Life and Death*)

The peacock named "Mr. Jackson" with Lady Lodge (from *Raymond, or Life and Death*)

vehicle on wheels that was used on the beach) and a pet peacock named "Mr. Jackson". In life Raymond knew the peacock, and the peacock died after Raymond was killed, but from the "afterlife" Raymond seemed to be aware that the peacock had died. In each of these cases the purported "Raymond" imparted information that was known to immediate family members, but not to the medium conducting the séance. However, such evidence only goes so far in establishing that it really was Raymond communicating from the "other side" through the medium. Another possibility, which must be seriously considered if one accepts the reality of telepathy (as Sir Oliver Lodge did), is that the medium was picking up conscious or unconscious thoughts on the part of still living family members and friends.

A particularly interesting case involved two séances held simultaneously. A brother and sister of Raymond's, Lionel and Norah, were attempting to communicate with Raymond via a medium in London. Another brother, Alec, at the time in Birmingham, knew about the séance that was taking place in London. Suddenly it occurred to Alec to try an experiment. He hastily gathered a couple of people together and carried out a short séance during which he asked Raymond to communicate the word "Honolulu" to Lionel and Norah during their séance. Those in London, knowing nothing of this plan, reported that Raymond (through the medium) had asked Norah if she could play a song titled "Honolulu". The experiment was a success and in the opinion of the family helped establish the reality of Raymond in the afterlife and their communications with him. Of course, in this case once again, it could be argued that the word "Honolulu" was somehow transmitted telepathically from Alec to the medium who was conducting the séance with Lionel and Norah. Sir Oliver Lodge considered this possibility; however, many find telepathy between living humans a less probable explanation and prefer to believe that spirits on the other side do indeed exist and can receive and transmit messages.

Perhaps the most compelling evidence for the reality of the otherworldly Raymond involved a photograph of a group of officers, including Raymond, taken on the Front on 24 August 1915 just a few weeks prior to Raymond's death. The family first learned from the spirit form of Raymond, during a séance on 27 September 1915, that such a photograph had been taken. Sir Oliver Lodge made inquiries about the photograph, but came up empty-handed. However, Lady Lodge received a letter on 29 November 1915 from Mrs. B. P. Cheves, whose son had known Raymond, asking if the family would like a copy of a photograph of a group of officers taken in August 1915 that, presumably, included Raymond. Prior to the photograph's arrival, during a séance held on 3 December 1915, Raymond was questioned directly about the photograph. He described it to the best of his ability, various details of which were confirmed once the photograph arrived in the hands of the Lodge family on 7 December 1915. Details seen in the photograph, and previously described by Raymond during the séance, included the

Photograph of a group of officers taken on 24 August 1915; Raymond Lodge is sitting in the front row, second from the right (from *Raymond, or Life and Death*)

fact that it was a mixed bunch of officers from different Companies grouped closely together, that some were standing in the back, some were sitting (including Raymond, who appears in the front row, second from the right), that he had a walking stick (mentioned with the first notice of the photograph during a séance on 27 September 1915), that it was taken outdoors apparently in front of a shelter, there was a pattern of vertical and horizontal lines behind the group (which in the photograph is seen in the roof and walls of the shelter before which the group posed), and that someone was leaning on him or putting pressure on him (it can be seen in the photograph that the officer behind Raymond is resting his hand and arm on Raymond's shoulder).

In the case of the photograph, no one at the séance (and virtually no one on the planet) knew the details of the photograph at the time Raymond described them. These were only confirmed afterwards upon receipt of the photo. Excluding simple coincidence, which seems highly unlikely, three major possibilities might explain this situation: 1) a form of precognition during which the medium, or members of the family who then transmitted the precognized information to the medium, picked up information from the future viewing of the photograph, 2) telepathic information was somehow received directly by the medium from someone who had seen the photograph, or perhaps from the photographer, despite being unknown to the medium and members of the Lodge family, or 3) that Raymond really did exist in an afterlife state and relayed accurate details regarding the photograph. If we accept, with Sir Oliver Lodge, the third explanation as the most likely, this can be regarded as strong evidence for life after death.

What do we make of *Raymond, or Life and Death* nearly a century later? I just do not know. I am convinced that Sir Oliver Lodge was a brilliant scientist, and even while investigating the case for survival of his own son in an "afterlife" he did not suspend his critical judgment or abandon his search for solid evidence. He took precautions against fraud and self-deception. He concluded that there is an afterlife, at least of some form. In his book *Raymond* Sir Oliver Lodge suggests that the spirit world may be found in the realm of thought, stating:

> ... telepathy proves that bodily organs are not absolutely essential to communication of ideas.[5] Mind turns out to be able to act directly on mind . . . Thought does not belong to the material region; although it is able to exert an influence on that region . . . It is reasonable to suppose that the mind can be more at home, and more directly and more exuberantly active, where the need for such interaction . . . [with the material world] . . . no longer exists, when the restraining influence of brain and nerve mechanism is removed, and when some of the limitations connected with bodily location in space are ended.[6]

The Nature and Basis of Consciousness

But what is thought and mind? I suggest that in this context thought is equivalent to, or one and the same as, consciousness. This brings us to the very questions we opened this essay with: What is mind? What is thought? What is consciousness? Are mind, thought, and consciousness simply electrochemical manifestations of the conglomeration of our nervous tissue, or are they something more, something independent of our current material form?

The usual general status quo materialistic position is that "obviously" mind, thought, consciousness — whatever terms one decides to use — are epiphenomenona that arise from the material world, and the "hard problem" is to explain the physical origin of consciousness, subtleties of conscious experience and thought, which for most conscious beings pondering such perplexities includes the notion of free will. This is in contrast to the "easy problem" which has been characterized as follows by Stuart Hameroff (The University of Arizona Medical Center, Tucson, Arizona) and Deepak Chopra (The Chopra Center, Carlsbad, California):

> The prevalent modern scientific approach to consciousness casts the brain as a biological computer, with 100 billion neurons and their axonal firings and synaptic connections acting as information networks of 'bit' states and switches. Variability in synaptic strengths mediated by chemical neurotransmitters shapes network activity and enables learning and intelligent functions . . . . This 'brain-as-computer' view is able to account for complex nonconscious cognitive functions including perception and control of behavior. Such nonconscious cognitive functions are described as 'zombie modes,' 'auto-pilot,' or 'easy problems'. . . . The 'easiness' derives from the apparent cause-and-effect between specific computational functions of brain neurons, and actions and behavior which do not involve conscious will or phenomenal experience.[7]

Taking this approach to an extreme, one could view apparent evidence of consciousness in some object – be it a rabbit or a fellow human – as effectively and simply automated responses to stimuli. Perhaps there is no such thing as consciousness, including in you. Perhaps it is all a cruel trick, an illusion. But is it an illusion that has been made known to us? An illusion of which we are now conscious? But supposed consciousness of the illusion is simply an automated response, and not true consciousness. And on and on and on... To simply dismiss the notion of consciousness in this way is not very satisfying to the typical conscious being who may feel quite certain that she or he is indeed genuinely conscious. Yet the standard materialist approach to consciousness, which adopts the "thesis that matter is primary and consciousness secondarily emergent from it",[8] appears to have at best set up a smokescreen to hide the lack of delivery of a cogent explanation of the source of consciousness in the material world. "Despite detailed understanding of neuronal firings, synaptic transmissions, neurotransmitter chemistry, and neuronal computation, there is no accounting for conscious experience, the 'self,' free will or 'qualia' – the essence of experienced perceptions."[9] In an essay titled "Is Consciousness Primary?", after a lengthy analysis of the materialistic approach, Michel Bitbol (Ecole Polytechnique, Paris) writes:

> At this point, we have almost reached our conclusion. Consciousness is *existentially, transcendentally,* and *methodologically* primary. Any attempt at showing how it can be *ontologically secondary* to material objects both fails and draws us back to its methodological primacy.[10]

So maybe we need to turn the materialistic approach on its head, up side down, and consider that thought and consciousness are primary. But if so, where do they originate? Where do they come from? Or are these the wrong questions to ask? Rather than consciousness being illusionary, as some extreme materialists would contend, perhaps it is the other way around. Consciousness may be all that there is, in an ultimate sense, and the material world of matter and energy is simply an illusion created by consciousness. This latter approach is sometimes referred to as "idealism" as opposed to "materialism". The idealist approach is often associated, rightfully or wrongly, with religion and religious beliefs (is the ultimate consciousness "God" or the "Creator"?) as opposed to the "scientific" (and perhaps, or some would say necessarily, atheistic) approach of materialism.

But must we pick between these two extremes, between materialism and idealism? Not according to Stuart Hameroff and British physicist Sir Roger Penrose (University of Oxford). They advocate a third approach, which can be summarized as follows:

> *Consciousness results from discrete physical events; such events have* *always existed in the universe as non-cognitive, proto-conscious events,* *these acting as part of precise physical laws not yet fully understood.* Biology evolved a mechanism to orchestrate such events and to couple them to neuronal activity, resulting in meaningful, cognitive, conscious moments and thence also to causal control of behavior. These events are proposed specifically to be moments of quantum state reduction (intrinsic quantum 'self-measurement'). Such events need not necessarily be taken as part of current theories of the laws of the universe, but should ultimately be scientifically describable.[11]

The sub-microscopic quantum world is very different from the macroscopic "classical" world of everyday common experience. At the risk of oversimplifying, we can say that at the quantum level particles can act as waves, and vice versa, and can exist in multiple states and places simultaneously. This is often referred to as quantum superposition, which can be thought of as co-existing possibilities for a particle/wave or set of particles/waves. Furthermore, particles can become entangled, become parts of a system, and remain entangled even after they are separated spatially. An added twist is that at the quantum level it seems the past and the future blend together, or form a fuzzy region wherein the past and the future (as we think of them) are not distinct and separable, and the future can influence the past as well as the past influencing the future.[12]

In the "real" (real to most people, that is) or everyday world of macroscopic objects we do not observe superpositions and entanglements, but discrete material objects in space and time (for instance, an object sitting at rest or moving at some velocity). It seems that when quantum systems are measured or observed the probabilistic quantum wave function is "collapsed" or "reduced" to a definite state, a state that is "chosen" from the different possible states. Why this occurs is commonly known as the "measurement problem",[13] and how it is interpreted remains an issue. One possibility, proposed by pioneer quantum physicist Niels Bohr (and since known as the Copenhagen interpretation) is that conscious observation results in the collapse of the wave function, in the reduction of the possibilities to one definite state. In this view, consciousness is external to the system (and ultimately to the universe as we know it as a system at the largest scale?) and it is this external (and fundamental?) consciousness that causes quantum state reduction. In this manner one might argue that consciousness is primary or fundamental or even beyond universal. But does this explain consciousness, or simply put the problem off to a different realm, perhaps a realm that is beyond science and rational thought? This itself seems to be a paradox if such really is the case (whatever "really" should mean).

Another interpretation, which in some ways to me seems to avoid the issue of consciousness, or turns it into an illusion (thus reverting to a strong materialistic approach), is that there effectively is no single reduction to a definite state. Rather at each quantum superposition all of the possibilities are expressed, all the possible states, but in different and presumably coexisting universes. This multiple or many worlds view[14] would, in my assessment, include universes with the illusion of consciousness (and presumably we live in such a universe) – though one might ask where the illusion begins and ends; can the illusion of consciousness result in true consciousness? – as well as universes lacking consciousness in any form. Ultimately, by this interpretation, all possibilities are realized.

Not actual state reduction or collapse of the wave function in a technical sense, but related to these issues, is decoherence. Theoretical physicist Wojciech H. Zurek has described decoherence in the following manner:

> Macroscopic systems are never isolated from their environments. Therefore . . . they should not be expected to follow Schrödinger's equation [describing the wave function; how the quantum state of a system changes with time], which is applicable only to a closed system. As a result, systems usually regarded as classical suffer (or benefit) from the natural loss of quantum coherence, which 'leaks out' into the environment . . . . The resulting 'decoherence' cannot be ignored when one addresses the problem of the reduction of the quantum mechanical wave packet: Decoherence imposes, in effect, the required 'embargo' on the potential outcomes by allowing the observer to maintain records of alternatives but to be aware of only one of the branches – one of the 'decoherent histories'...[15]

In my view, decoherence is certainly important but it does not ultimately explain quantum reduction, as it only deals with quantum systems that are interacting with an external environment. But what about a self-contained and isolated quantum system? Does it undergo reduction? Or are their no isolated quantum systems, which would mean that quantum systems are not fundamental or primary, which could lead us back to the concept that perhaps the reason there are no truly isolated quantum systems that we are aware of is due to the external influence of consciousness which is outside of, or external to, any quantum system. Does this take us back to the concept that consciousness (or conscious observation) collapses or reduces quantum possibilities to definite states?

Another approach to the issue of quantum state reduction is commonly referred to as "objective reduction (OR)" wherein "specific objective thresholds cause quantum state reduction".[16] Sir Roger Penrose has developed and elaborated upon a particular theory of objective reduction, often referred to as Diósi-Penrose objective reduction, as the work of the Hungarian physicist Lajos Diósi has contributed to this theory. According to this line of thinking, using a crude analogy, a quantum particle can be represented as causing a curvature in space-time, and prior to reduction it will cause multiple simultaneous curvatures in different directions, representing different locations where it might occur. Thus "a separation, bubble, or blister in the very fabric of reality" will form.[17] However, this is not a situation that can be sustained. "Penrose has suggested that such space-time separations are unstable and will reduce, or collapse to one particular state or location at a particular time due to an objective threshold intrinsic to the fine structure of the universe, like infinitesimally tiny soap bubbles bursting one facet or another, shaping and creating a new reality."[18] A different analogy, one that I will suggest here, is that of a perfectly homogeneous rubber band. As the rubber band is stretched and stretched (representing the evolution of the quantum states and superpositions with time), eventually it will snap (the reduction of the quantum state to a definite state). Given that the rubber band is perfectly homogeneous, there will be a random aspect to the final state arrived at during this objective reduction. If the rubber band has inhomogeneities or other influences on it, the reduction will not be fully random.

What does all of this have to do with the topic at hand, the nature of consciousness? Remember the "measurement problem", one solution of which calls for consciousness to be external to the quantum system so as to do the measuring and trigger the reduction. The opposite is the case according to the theory of Diósi-Penrose objective reduction: "Rather, the DP [Diósi-Penrose] proposal suggests each OR [objective reduction] event, which is a purely physical process, is itself a primitive kind of 'observation', a moment of 'proto-conscious experience'."[19] If this is correct, then consciousness arises from quantum level reduction at the boundary between the quantum world and the macroscopic classical world. Consciousness (or proto-consciousness) is inherent, intrinsic, to the universe as we know it. It is neither a mere epiphenomenonal illusion nor something imposed on the universe from some unknown "outside" region.

In my rubber band analogy above, I suggested that if the rubber band is perfectly homogeneous, then the objective reduction event should be random relative to the possibilities (represented by points along the length of the stretched rubber band). But if the rubber band is not perfectly homogeneous, then the probabilities of snapping in one place or another will not be the same. Penrose, in his analysis, suggests that this is the case and objective reduction is not random, "but influenced by information embedded in fundamental space-time geometry, information Penrose characterized as Platonic values . . . . The Greek philosopher Plato described an abstract world of pure form, mathematical truth, and ethical and aesthetic values. Penrose suggests such Platonic values, along with precursors of physical laws, constants, forces, and consciousness, literally *exist* as patterns in fundamental space-time, encoded in Planck scale [that is, at the quantum level] geometry."[20]

Diósi-Penrose objective reduction resulting in moments of proto-consciousness is not, apparently, the equivalent of full-scale consciousness as we humans know it. Together Penrose and Hameroff have developed the theory of orchestrated objective reduction (Orch OR) to account for consciousness as we experience it.[21] Essentially, orchestrated coherent series of quantum reductions result in moments and sequences of consciousness and choice or decision-making.

For humans and higher animals, and apparently (according to the Penrose and Hameroff theory) in other eukaryotic organisms as well, this orchestrated objective reduction takes place in the microtubules of the cellular cytoskeleton (and particularly in the microtubules within brain neurons of humans and higher animals).

Without going too deeply into the subject, or getting bogged down with equations, the Diósi-Penrose proposal suggests that "superposition reduces to one of the alternatives in a timescale τ that can be estimated (for a superposition of two states each of which is assumed to be taken to be stationary on its own) according to the formula $\tau \approx \hbar / E_G$"[22] where $\hbar$ is Planck's constant divided by 2π and "E_G is the *gravitational self-energy* of the *difference* between the two (stationary) mass distributions of the superposition".[23] Various studies and data sets, from electro-encephalography (EEG) to Buddhist meditation, suggest that typical human consciousness is actually a series of discrete events, like the frames of a movie, with about 30 to 90 moments of consciousness per second (30 to 90 Hz [Hertz]).[24] According to the calculations of Hameroff and Penrose, based on the properties of microtubules and other factors, these rates of moments of consciousness are comparable to those predicted by their hypothesis of orchestrated objective reduction occurring in microtubules within human brain neurons. (As a side note, I hypothesize that a trained meditator may be able to modulate this frequency, perhaps to tap into various levels of "world" or "universal" moments of consciousness.)

Beyond microtubules in cells, there may be many other situations where orchestrated objective reduction occurs, giving rise to full-scale consciousness, perhaps on timescales that are rather alien to us and in non-biological contexts (non-biological as we know biology composed of carbon-based organisms requiring water). Hameroff and Penrose speculate that "it is certainly conceivable that sentient creatures might have evolved in parts of the universe that would be highly alien to us, for example on neutron-star surfaces."[25] Furthermore, they suggest, such entities might have orchestrated objective reduction events, thus conscious moments, at a rate a million times faster than that of a human. On the other end of the time scale, perhaps there are entities with consciousness, but their conscious moments are a million times (or more!) slower than in a human (my own speculation). Could a crystal or a nebula in outer space experience orchestrated objective reduction – that is, experience consciousness – but at the appropriate timeframe? Such a case can be cogently made, in my assessment. If such is the case, true consciousness may be a widespread, even universal, aspect of the cosmos and "everything" as we know it, based upon the proto-conscious events of objective reduction. The universe as a whole may be conscious.

Returning to humans in particular, even if the microtubules in the neurons of the brain are the primary physical locus of consciousness in our species, this does not preclude that our consciousness could spread further (beyond localization in the brain) in some cases. In this context, Hameroff and Chopra discuss the idea that consciousness at times may literally exist outside of the human body, for instance during near-death experiences, out-of-body experiences, and after death. Uniting all of these experiences is the fact that the physical brain is not in its "normal" state, whether under duress and dying physiologically, or being manipulated and altered via such means as meditation, stress, drugs, and so forth. This, they suggest, may explain the concept of a soul that is common to so many religions and cultures, and may also mean that a form of "afterlife" is literally possible. They write,

> In the Orch OR [Orchestrated Objective Reduction] context, consciousness occurs as a process at the level of fundamental space-time geometry. When the brain is under duress, it is conceivable quantum information processes constituting consciousness dissipate to the nonlocal universe at large. A dualist perspective, in which a separate, as yet undefined

spiritual information field constitutes awareness outside the body, may not be necessary. An afterlife, an actual soul-as-quantum information leaving the body and persisting as entangled fluctuations in multiple scales, or planes in quantum space-time geometry, may be scientifically possible.[26]

If this is possible for humans, then it seems to me that it is possible for non-human conscious beings (even non-biological entities possessing consciousness, if such exist, as I suspect they do). Perhaps all consciousness persists.

SPECULATIONS

Taking the ideas above, and placing my own interpretations on them, I will here speculate further regarding the nature of consciousness and ultimately the universe as we know it.

I do not view the following concepts as mutually exclusive: orchestrated objective reduction, decoherence, and the reduction of the quantum wave function (also sometimes referred to as "collapse of the state vector") due to conscious observations. All may have their part to play in the shaping of consciousness and the manifestation of the universe as we know it.

Consciousness may arise, in an ultimate sense, from random or chaotic quantum superpositions that collapse and are reduced to discrete states in a coordinated, collated, or orchestrated manner. Once consciousness arises from such reduction, the consciousness itself can now serve as an observer, as a catalyst, as a "measurer" to foment and instigate, to cause, further reduction; but such reduction will now be less random and reinforce previous reductions. Whereas initially there was more randomness among the reductions, more randomness among the conscious moments, as more consciousness moments accumulate and are experienced, these will tend to follow the path of previous conscious moments ("previous" being used somewhat metaphorically here, as the question of time is a subject of debate and initially at least there may have been no distinguishable past and future, such concepts only resulting from an agreement among conscious moments). The end result will manifest as a relatively consistent universe[27] – consistent in terms of the basic "laws" of physics and nature at large, consistent in the nature of what we term matter and energy, and so forth. Essentially, of the possible superpositions available in the quantum world, some will become increasingly common due to precedent and the observer effect directing reduction along certain paths. However, there will always remain the possibility (if not probability) of other paths of reduction and thus a level of randomness that cannot be fully eliminated. This may tie in with the "irrationality" and "trickster" aspects of various parapsychological and paranormal phenomena, phenomena that have been suppressed to a great extent in some societies and cultures by a consensus that such phenomena should not or cannot exist.

Given the quantum level basis of consciousness, I suspect that all consciousness is to a greater or lesser extent entangled. Whether we care to acknowledge it or not, the universe we inhabit is enacted and constructed by consciousnesses; it is a collective endeavor. This gives the world a certain consistency and commonality from one being and consciousness to another. Two different people may "see" the world ever so slightly differently, but in the main most people experience primarily the same world, that which is often considered "objective reality" composed of matter and energy. But there is nothing ultimately objective about it, other than that it is more or less agreed upon by the conscious beings who have created such an "objective reality" which exists now at a subconscious and unconscious as well as conscious level. Indeed, not acknowledging that this is the case is part of the shared consensus that perpetuates the relatively consistent world we inhabit together.

Decoherence may also play a role, indeed a large role, in the shaping of the world (universe) as we know it. As consciousness constructs, through directed reduction, a consistent universe, then this now macroscopic and manifested matter-energy, space-time, universe will erode the coherence of quantum systems. It will instigate leakage and decoherence from the fundamental quantum systems, and indeed drive them to reduce along lines compatible with the already existing macroscopic "classical" construction of the developing universe. Precedent will play a large role (as well as entanglement), and this may be manifested at many levels, from the structure of matter and energy to parapsychological consistency (I think of the "morphic resonances" discussed by Rupert Sheldrake[28]).

When it comes right down to it, consciousness is not bound by space and time, but creates space and time. At quantum scales, the scales from which consciousness originates, the past and the future abut against each other and form a fuzzy boundary. There may be no limit to the intermingling of what we perceive as the past and the future and our perceptual reality is on the edge of what has been and what is to come. But it must be stressed that the very notion of a flow of time, past and future, is simply a construct of consciousness. We as conscious entities create a shared and consistent "reality" with spatial and temporal coordinates to keep us from "going insane". Consciousness, and the "reality" consciousness creates, stands at the boundary between the quantum world and the classical macroscopic world of everyday experiences. Consciousness is the interface and connection between these two worlds. The world of everyday experiences, "objective" reality, of mind, space, and time, cannot exist without consciousness. Indeed the world only exists because of consciousness.

If we accept, at least for heuristic purposes, that consciousness originates in quantum processes, then one can argue we have simply pushed the question of the origin of consciousness back one level. Where did the quantum world, the quantum entities, come from in the first place? Perhaps the most honest answer is that we simply do not know, but we can speculate. A vacuum, a quantum vacuum or zero-point field, is not really a vacuum at all but rather a plenum of particle pairs or virtual particles (particles and their anti-particles) appearing and disappearing, spontaneously created and annihilated once again. Such quantum fluctuations occur in a vacuum (as predicted by the uncertainty principle of quantum mechanics) and the objective reduction of a quantum superposition spontaneously created from or within a vacuum could have been the first conscious moment and effectively seeded the universe for more such events, resulting in the creation of both the universe and consciousness as we know them.

We began this essay with a recounting of the British physicist Sir Oliver Lodge and his apparent communications with his deceased son Raymond who was killed on the front lines in 1915. Sir Oliver Lodge concluded that "Thought does not belong to the material region; although it is able to exert an influence on that region . . ." He was writing in 1916, and at that time quantum theory was still in its infancy and most of the quantum mechanical concepts we have touched on here had not yet been developed. Furthermore, Lodge was committed to a different physics, the physics of the ether.[29] Still, if Lodge were with us today, I wonder how he might view this discussion. He might even agree that thought, that consciousness, not only does not belong to the material realm, but created the material realm and thus can and does influence the world of matter and energy.

In the beginning was a proto-conscious moment, in the beginning was a thought, "In the beginning was the Word"...[30]

Robert M. Schoch received his Ph.D. in Geology and Geophysics from Yale University. Since 1984 he has been a full-time faculty member at the College of General Studies of Boston University. The author of numerous works, his most recent book is *Forgotten Civilization: The Role of Solar Outbursts in Our Past and Future* (Inner Traditions, 2012). Dr. Schoch's personal website is www.robertschoch.com.

Egyptian Bull Mummy Mask (Gryffindor, Creative Commons Share Alike)

CULT OF THE
COSMIC BULL

LINKING THE THOUGHT-WORLDS OF NABTA PLAYA, LASCAUX, AND GÖBEKLI TEPE

by *Alistair Coombs*

People familiar with the adventures of G.I. Gurdjieff may recall his 'map of pre-sand Egypt', said to have been purloined from an Armenian priest in the region of south-east Anatolia. Though doubts about the map may be warranted, given the fantastical nature of its source – Gurdjieff's own autobiography, *Meetings with Remarkable Men* – the staggering antiquity of recently excavated sites of that region could offer some support for the idea that Gurdjieff's mysterious cartographic document was genuine. The geological record of north-east Africa, for instance, has indeed borne witness to oscillating climatic conditions, marked by a fluctuation between hyper-arid and rainy conditions over a 260,000 year period. During extended wet periods, the Egyptian Sahara took the form of a savannah, replete with many species of flora and fauna – including *Bos primigenius*, more commonly known as aurochs (the wild and burly ancestor of domesticated cattle).

Located 100 kilometres west of the pharaonic monuments of Abu Simbel, Nabta Playa is the wadi, or basin, of a large lake that has since naturally drained away. Nabta appears to have been abandoned and re-occupied several times in the period since 11,000 BCE, due to alternating surges of hyper-aridity and flooding. The first settlers of the region may have arrived from the Makhadma site in the Nile Valley, itself inhabited from 11,300-10,000 BCE.[1] It is suspected that exchange between Neolithic Nile Valley groups and the Saharan pastoralists inhabiting the Nabta Playa region – whoever these people were and from wherever they came – formed the nucleus from which Egypt's epoch of high culture would later emerge. Quite how this occurred, however, remains a mystery. Certainly though, remains excavated at Nabta do seem to reveal an early source from which the religious (specifically, mortuary) beliefs of the Egyptians flourished, and to which the monumentality of later Egyptian art and architecture remained closely aligned.

For instance, a complex located on the western edge of the Nabta wadi reveals a series of ceremonial stone-covered tumuli with clay-lined stone and tamarisk roofed-chambers which together mark an aurochs burial site, and has been dated to the 6th millennium BCE.[2] Skeletal remains that have been uncovered show the beasts were ceremonially buried in a north-south alignment, with their heads facing south. Other sites outside of Nabta and of a later date, such as those in the el-Badari region, show evidence of mature-age aurochs being interred in close proximity to human burials, and sometimes even together with humans – a tradition which continued down to pre-dynastic and Old Kingdom times, alongside a developing bull-ritual iconography such as that located at Hierakonpolis. These practices at Nabta reflect neolithic European burials, where bull bones have been found in barrows in conjunction with human remains, as well as in ritual burials where the hide of a bull with its hooves and horns would have hung directly above the deceased.

Egyptian mythology that has the bull as the first primordial god, the first gods being bulls, and the pharaoh, rulers and men, evolving from the bull, appears to originate from Nabta Playa. The undomesticated auroch stood some seven feet high, and with its broad sky-scraping horns it is small wonder why this beast excited early religious imaginations. From pre-dynastic times onward, themes connecting bulls with kings are deeply embedded and numerous in example. In later times, for instance, a sarcophagus in the Khafre pyramid at Giza was discovered to contain the bones of a bull, while Khufu – the pharaoh associated with the Great Pyramid – was known as 'the great wild bull' following earlier identifications of kings as such in the Pyramid Texts. But while bull-genesis mythology might be considered a likely widespread practice – after all, many cultures relied on these beasts for subsistence – if we look at the artistic resonances between east Saharan rock paintings, and Magdalenian bull art, we might start to wonder if the bull mythologies of these two already-ancient cultures shared their origin with an even earlier cult...

Furthermore, the circumstances of Nabta Playa also resonate with recently excavated sites in Anatolia (modern Turkey). Both regions were formerly lush verdant landscapes rich in vegetation and other food-sources – a hunter-gatherer's paradise. To both peoples, as to others of prehistory, the bull was not only a walking department-store – furnishing everything from clothing to food – but also an enchanted entity, venerated as a primal cosmic power. And evidence from both regions questions, in different

Nabta Stone Circle

ways, the conventional scheme of when the Neolithic shift into agriculture actually occurred.

Both these early peoples also appear to have possessed an astounding level of astronomical knowledge. Besides the occupational layers of planned housing located at Nabta (circa 9000-8800 BCE), there have been other artefacts, ceremonial remains, and subterranean and surface complexes uncovered, including a megalithic calendar circle and a smaller 'star clock' located within the basin of the lake. Extensive research by Thomas Brophy[3] has suggested that the calendar circle not only tracks annual celestial events, but also aligns with the belt stars of Orion at specific points in the cycle of precession (the 'wobble' of the Earth on its axis, like a spinning top, which over a 26,000 year period makes the positions of the stars in the sky shift). Furthermore, Brophy claims that the date 16,500 BCE is encoded within the astronomy of the circle, perhaps commemorating the arrival in the region of the mythical 'Shemsu-Hor' lineage: a group of sub-Saharan herders and astronomer-priests celebrated for the founding of Heliopolis, the 'City of the Sun' – perhaps the oldest city of Egypt. An inscription in one of the crypts at Dendera also states that the temple, along with its famous zodiac, was built according to plans set down on a goatskin parchment from the time of this ancestral cult. Perhaps more interestingly though, we also find that 16,500 BCE marks a highly significant date for the bull ritual in another part of the world, namely the Dordogne region of Lascaux, France.

SKY MAPS

Across the ancient world, both in the northern and southern hemispheres, most of the major gods had their abode in the Orion-Taurus-Pleiades region of sky. The drama of life, death, world cataclysm and its ultimate renewal was largely written across this legendary patch of sky, a veritable treasure chest of ancient religious and mythological ideas buried within its starry configurations.

Located in the neck of the Heavenly Bull lies the star cluster of the Pleiades. Following the festival of inundation of Dynastic Egypt (in which the star Sirius heralded the annual flooding of the Nile), the setting of this cluster marked the Khoiak festival, which revolved around the myth of the resurrected god Osiris.[4] These closely-grouped stars also became identified with the 'Seven Hathors' (or Fates) who oversaw birth and prophecy. One of their names captures a glimpse of the 'missing Pleiad' of later Greek fame, under her title 'the hidden one'. They also appear as seven asps in a later Mithraic liturgy, who acted as celestial consortia to seven males wearing bull-masks, echoing the Vedic myths of the Krittika (the ancient Indian interpretation of the Pleiades as a group of sisters) being wedded to the seven sages of Ursa Major. These are the fairly common (and oft-debated) mythological associations of these stars. However, they also appear to be incorporated in a far earlier stratum of Egyptian funerary myth and rite – one which may seem bizarre to us today but which would have made sense to the ancient Egyptians concerned with the cycle of life, in both the seasonal and individual sense.

The famous cave paintings of the 'Hall of Bulls' at Lascaux also indicate that Taurus and the Pleiades have been of interest since

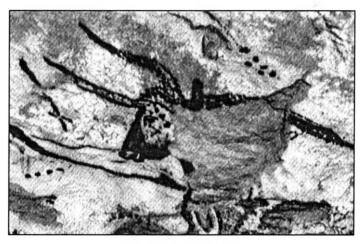

Lascaux bull and 'Pleiades'

Palaeolithic times – the fabulous art of this location usually being dated to around 16,500 B.C. – and confirms that the Taurus constellation was identified by these people also as a bull. At Lascaux the presence of the Pleiades may well signal their importance for reckoning the seasonal calendar of aurochs, marking cycles of breeding and hunting and perhaps more besides. As seasonal markers the Pleiades since Paleolithic times have opened the ritual calendar, signaled hunter-gatherer and agriculturalist activities, and provided an orientation in the cosmos, whilst their setting was a basis for festivals of the dead. Moreover, there is evidence to suggest that the rising and setting of the Pleiades, in combination with Taurus, marked the two seasons of a primitive year, one that predated the introduction of a lunar calendar. This is supported at sites such as Nabta Playa, Lascaux and Gobekli Tepe.

The inner chamber, or 'shaft of the dead man', at the Lascaux labyrinth reveals other arcana to which we will return.

Bones of the Stars

Looking back to Nabta Playa, we find a chain of ideas deeply embedded in the Egyptian psyche which is reflected in the Orion-Taurus-Pleiades constellations concerning life, death, and return – the Osirian influence. In later iconography we find these concepts embodied in the ritual implements of the Djed, Ankh, and Ureas; items that have a primal affiliation with the spine of a bull and which owe their cultic images to segments of it very directly.

In support of this, Calvin Schwabe *et al* have found an ancient stratum of belief involving 'semen' being produced within the spine of the bull, in particular the thoracic section.[5] Many Egyptian mortuary beliefs can be traced back to this sperm-spine complex. Texts from the Old Kingdom onward reference the neck, spine and tail of the bull in ways which portray their importance in the revivification of

Representations of the *Djed* pillar in Egyptian art

the dead. This ancient belief concerning semen ('life-power') being produced in the spine, within the marrow or cerebrospinal fluid, was not confined to Egypt, but was held across Africa, the Middle-East, and within Asia. In fact, it was an idea that didn't diminish until the time of Roman medical investigation, which advocated the testes as the sole sperm-producer rather than the spine. As such, the belief may throw light on otherwise obscure ancient symbolism and rituals, particularly ones involving bones, snakes and rebirth.

Attention placed on the bull's spine, the neck or thoracic section in ancient myths correlates with a celestial template: the position of the Pleiades within the neck of the heavenly bull. In Egyptian thinking, we often find the concerns and events of the physical world to outflow into the mythical, to colour the details and activities of the afterlife. Emphasis on the neck of the heavenly bull would have embodied a practical observation, since the annual movement of the Pleiades regulated the seasonal flow of cattle, governing their life-cycle by signalling the rains which produced the pastures sustaining them.

There is also ritualistic detail concerning the fastening of life-power in the neck's vertebral bones, more specifically either the soft interior marrow or cerebrospinal fluid, where the mysterious continuity of existence or power of Osiris was thought to reside – important not only for ongoing cycles of fertility, but also for ensuring successful emergence in the afterlife. The following passages indicate how the Pleiades are reflected in mortuary traditions, and are symbolised variously as serpents, cords, vertebrae, and knots, a symbology ascribed to them in other traditions:

> The king is a serpent, the Bull who leads, who swallowed his seven uraei and his seven neck-vertebrae came into being...[6]

A virtual repeat of the same from Spell 374 of the Coffin Texts:

> I am a snake... who swallowed his seven uraei, and his seven neck-vertebrae came into being.

And of the same theme:

> O you who knot your rope... O ferryman... O you seven knots of the celestial kine, I know you and I know your names, may you make me hale, you make my bones and my members hale.[7]

An earlier form of the Egyptian goddess Bat, and the sky-goddess Nut, was Mehet-Weret. In spell 691 of the Coffin Texts we initially find her addressed in plural as the 'celestial cattle', then later on in the spell as 'seven knots' (*thesu*). Toward the close of the spell, she appeals to a one-faced lord: "...may you destine me to annual life",[8] perhaps in reference to her earthly offspring, the annual birth of calves.

In the mortuary literature, a snake is conceived traversing the interior of the spine with the gods pulling him through the tail and out of the head of the bull, where he is reborn daily as the sun. We observe this configuration resulting in the Ureaus snake residing upon the brow of statuary, which would also have been influenced by a snake resembling the spinal cord of a bull – and that of a human by extension. We hear of the interior path of the bull's spine as the path or way of the dead, where takes place the union of the Ka and Ba after death:

> ... the road of the nau-snake, the bull of the sky, the bestower of powers, shall be cleared for me.[9]

Seeing that the mysterious life-power of existence was generated within the spine, the phallus was seen, quite literally, to be an anatomical extension of the spine from where life flowed. There are also indications that a celestial reconstruction of the body emphasising the spine and head (as reflected later in the Osirian dismemberment myth) preceded mummification, although it is difficult to estimate what this scenario might have entailed in practical terms. We also encounter liturgical references indicating that broths were made from bones, and that bones were smashed to extract the essence and spinal cord, presumably so the Pharaoh-bull-god could absorb the power of the 'spine of Osiris' via ceremonially sacrificed cattle.

Whether interpreted as literal or symbolic, the idea was widespread across the ancient world. In the Mithraic tradition, for instance, the Pleiades 'spot' is where the dagger is plunged into the neck of the

Mithras slaying the bull

sacrificial bull, a tradition which survives in sullied form even today
through the Roman heritage of the Spanish bullfight.

Near Eastern Sky-Bulls

It should be emphasised that, as within the Egyptian sphere, bull gods
were not primarily associated with the wild rolling plains of earth, but
with the sky. Their primary abode in sky mythologies is well attested
across the near east and Fertile Crescent. The twelve signs of the
zodiac for instance were collectively referred to by Sumerians as the
'shiny herd'. De Santillana and Von Dechend[10] connect the shaman's
sky-drum with the Mesopotamian lilissu drum, the cover of which
necessarily had to come from the hide of a black bull – a hide, moreover,
that was said to have the seven stars of the Pleiades on its forehead, so
emblematic of Taurus and sometimes of the supreme sky-god, Anu,
himself. This doesn't mean to say that Taurus was always identified
as a zodiacal constellation, or that all sky-bulls were identified with
Taurus, although the highly distinctive V-shaped appearance of this
constellation – apparently recognised since Palaeolithic times – likely
provided the archetype of such sky-mapping innovation. (Another
reason for the worship of the bull, specifically Taurus, across the
ancient world was likely due to the Taurid meteor shower unleashing
streams of brilliant fireballs, some even impacting to earth, and seen
to emanate from this constellation.)

Mesopotamian tradition also has bull-men raising the sun on
a sky-pole. The Sumerian Ikshur and later Assyrian Adad, gods of
thunder and the storm, were both primarily associated with bulls.
The Hurrian god of sky and lightning, Teshub, similarly had the bull
as his signature animal. Teshub's chariot was driven by the two sky
bulls Seri and Hurri ('day' and 'night' respectively) and given the task
of holding aloft planetary bodies. Later, we of course find the winged
Kabiri bulls of the Phrygian mystery tradition.

As an ancient concept the bull symbolised the universe, or more precisely the colossal powers which drove it. The ceremonial slaying of this beast conceptualised cosmogenesis, the birth of the world, a scheme encountered less gorily today over the coffee table in the zero Trump/Tarot card of 'The Fool', or Aleph (meaning ox); that which is primal, beyond conception, from where the journey of the world begins.

GÖBEKLI TEPE – TEMPLE OF THE STAR BEASTS

"The bull is father to the snake and the snake to the bull."
- Dionysian Mysteries

Neolithic sites across Anatolia such as Çatalhüyük, Nevali Çori and Göbekli Tepe all lie within close vicinity of the Taurus Mountains, a designation which people as early as the Hurrians appear to have applied to this mountain range. The bull cult located at Çatalhüyük (c7500 BCE) is well-documented. And east of Göbekli Tepe lies Hallan Çemi, a less excavated site which may predate the former by a whole millennium, and at which an imposing bucranium has been uncovered which probably fulfilled ritualistic use.

Göbekli Tepe itself is something like the merging of an elaborate hunting-lodge, open-air feasting-hall, and naturalistic gallery of afterlife judgments: festooned with avian watchers, snakes, scorpions and bugs. In terms of architectural awe Göbekli Tepe may not measure up to other monuments across the ancient world, but in terms of antiquity, it towers above them. Its monumental age has it standing in the misty borderlands inhabited by lost continents. The site heaves with a strange spirituality which almost seems to condense from the air, as if one were standing in a crypt or catacomb. Interestingly enough a cave has been uncovered at the site, its interior decorated by a bull relief. Three things are certain about this site

The author standing beside one of the massive pillars of Göbekli Tepe

at this stage: firstly, that it has bloodied the nose of the idea of the Neolithic revolution and has earth-shaking ramifications for our understanding of human development; secondly, that it was a sanctuary where the living mingled with the dead; and thirdly, that its megalithic precincts served different capacities over the two millennia (or more) of their progressive construction and use.

The enclosures excavated thus far are built in ceremonial sphere-like structures, suggesting a reflection of the cosmos, as if their builders had an interest in the sky. And there is evidence that they did. Robert Schoch[11] has proposed that the builders of Göbekli Tepe were aware of precession, having discovered its effect at vernal equinoxes over the extended period of the site's habitation – from c10,000 BCE to 8500 BCE, when Orion-Taurus-Pleiades were visible before dawn from the direction of the chthonic twin-pillars that dominate each enclosure. The phenomenon of precession is based on a visual illusion caused by a 'wobble' in the Earth's axis – similar to the effect of a toppling gyroscope – which makes it appear (from Earth) that the sun, observed at twilight on a certain day each and every year (such as the equinox or solstice), regresses very slowly backward through the zodiac to its original 'starting point' along the ecliptic every 26,000 years (approximately).[12] Observation of the phenomenon of precession doesn't imply that one would necessarily be aware of the full 26,000 year cycle; but depending on the accuracy of the measuring method involved, the visual effect of precession could be observed in a much shorter duration, over a period of only 300-200 years.

Schoch's thinking is based on the curiously drifting trajectories of the enclosures of Layer III. At the present time, it is difficult to find an alternative explanation for the enclosures each being aligned progressively east of south, if they were not planned to mirror the Orion-Taurus-Pleiades region of sky – it appears they were 'chasing' these constellations under the offsetting tide of precession. It is unlikely that this is due to chance. Such a scenario would offer a credible explanation for the successively diminutive construction

Pillar 43 of Enclosure D (the 'Vulture-Stone') at Göbekli Tepe

behind the enclosures anterior to Enclosure D, as if their builders were attempting, in vain, to relink with the 'first time', which had since wandered across the heavens.

CORDS OF DEATH

One of the most fascinating frescoes at Göbekli Tepe is the one decorating the 'vulture-stone' (pillar 43) of Enclosure D, which could be a cosmograph or astrograph – something which is reproducing a geographical region of the sky. This is suggested by the central orb figure poised on the vulture's wing, which is quite possibly a depiction of the Sun. The three items lining the top of the stone appear like connected padlocks or baskets – and as the practice of basketry may have derived from watching the behaviour of birds making nests, this could well be so. However, I have a different theory: that these three joined items are intended to replicate a horizontal column of three vertebrae. The column's horizontal position, above what may be an afterlife scenario embedded within a cosmological depiction, is highly reminiscent of the backbone of Egypt's cow-star-goddess. While there are multiple afterlife locations indicated in Egyptian mortuary literature, the basic picture here appears similar to depictions of the goddess Bat – envisioned as the Milky Way – or the spine of Nut or Hathor, extending from the south to the circumpolar constellations. Secondly, about the column is what could be an enfolding layer flesh, complete with an eviscerated length of spinal cord below. Lastly, above the column (that is, on the right) is a knot, (see circled section of image opposite) which appears again as a 'pendant' within the central channel of pillar 28 (Enclosure C). This item is very similar in detail to three Egyptian hieroglyphs which mean both knot and

vertebrae (see image on the right) – the Ankh and 'knot of Isis' are variations – used for securing the life-power or cerebrospinal fluid within the bones, with a symbolism emblematic of undying life. The depiction of the headless ithyphallic man is also suggestively Osirian, and in looking at the scorpion it is perhaps significant that the solstice sun occupied the house of Scorpio during the period of construction of Enclosure D. There is also an astonishing resemblance between the vulture stone and astronomical depictions found on the 'old star path' (constellations that cluster round the galactic centre) of the Barasana zodiac, which lends further support to the idea that what is portrayed here is not an entirely subjective scene, but reflects a region of sky. The 'new star path' of the Barasana zodiac incorporates galactic anti-centre constellations such as the Pleiades which are the pivot of the year, an orientation which the central T-shapes appear to fulfill at this site.

HIDDEN GOD SNAKE

The geographical location of Göbekli Tepe has also seen it mentioned occasionally as the possible location of the Biblical Garden of Eden – which it may well be, at least in symbolic terms as the home of the Neolithic shift into agriculture. As such, given our discussion so far, it's worth recalling the puzzling story of Eve being created from a rib or thoracic bone from Adam.

The belief that bones retained magical fecundity or life-power (physically they are the vestiges of the dead that remain the longest) is well-attested at Göbekli Tepe, since bone refuse – notably, bones intentionally smashed to the marrow[13] – was a key ingredient of the backfill used to inundate the site. According to Klaus Schmidt, the archaeologist leading the excavations at the site, the backfilling formed part of a regular activity long before the site's final abandonment, and was possibly to do with a ritual of the dead involving bones.[14] Was this submersion in bone-saturated backfill intended to magically invigorate the site? Perhaps this was necessary in view of its sky guardians slowly deserting it by shifting across the sky. An indication of a shift from a stellar to a more 'steady' solar orientation at the site, for what ever reasons this may have been due, is that later enclosures apparently target the rising sun.

In Enclosure A on pillar 2 (see image on next page), we find what presents as an intentionally stylised aurochs relief. While there are not other examples of this type of depiction to compare with at present, it is difficult to see this aurochs as a realistic portrayal, which is the case with the other animals below and scattered across other friezes. Here, the artist appears to be adding significance to the bovine's extended cranial protuberance with the horns turned forward, as if the head were pregnant with a sun, so evocative of the pervasive Egyptian solar-bull.

In the earlier instances of bucrania, in Enclosure D the bull's cranium is comparatively triangular in shape and characteristic of the unusual appearance (if portrayed realistically) of snake crania at both Göbekli Tepe and Nevali Çori. This interesting artistic correspondence between the crania of bulls and snakes may not be coincidental, since on pillar 20 (Enclosure D) a bull and snake are peculiarly depicted head-to-head, as if altercating. It appears that out of the teeming taxonomy of beasts depicted across Layer III, there is, for some unknown reason, an enigmatic affinity implied between these two animals in particular.

Across the ancient world sacred animals such as the bull, usually when sacrificed, were consumed not only to sustain a diet but also to absorb their powers. We recall Yima's fall from divinity in this regard. The innards of an animal would also reveal a hidden, interior dimension of nature, and form the background to extispicy – the divination by means of impressions registered on the internal organs of an animal, such as was practiced later in Sumeria.

While we cannot at present infer anything like extispicy was practiced by the builders of Göbekli Tepe and related sites, we do find identities linked with animals deemed significant, or remains of them, relics which possibly served as the oracular ghost of the animal.

Pillar 2 of Enclosure A (the 'Solar Bull') at Göbekli Tepe

As in Egypt and other regions, a thorough familiarity of animal anatomy probably forewent knowledge of human anatomy. The size and likeness of the spinal cord of the bull (or human) compared to a snake would likely have provided a source of intrigue that forged symbolic connections, one that came to signify the hidden essence or 'spirit' of a person, perhaps a sort of Neolithic kundalini, something that indicated the mysterious matrix of renewal.

It is difficult to comprehend the numerous depictions of spermatozoon-like snakes that rove the pillars like surges of primal energy as entirely realistic interpretations, as we can with the majority of other fauna. They are clearly used ornamentally, though it may have been not in the purely decorative sense. Comparable to dragon iconography, snakes figure as semi-supernatural intermediaries in their portrait behaviour. Given their natural habitats, snakes are normally guardians of the underworld, but here they are shown trailing down pillars as if descending from the sky and flowing upward as if to return. On one pillar three snakes combine to produce a triple thunderbolt-like image, reminiscent of that wielded by Hurrian sky god Teshub.

On another pillar we find snakes merging with cranes and other avians, a vulture among them. Since this could not be a realistic scene, it's possible that it may be emphasising the elongated necks of the cranes and vultures with the body of the snake in abstract homologue. There are other instances of this nature. A detail on the vulture-stone shows the neck of a crane curiously transformed to a snake at its other end. Upon the 'totem pole' uncovered at Göbekli Tepe is a man's head depicted on the body of the snake ascending to the right of the sculpture. As in Mesoamerican combinations of snake and bird, these instances present sediments of thinking, motivated by a pattern of belief, one that would appear to prioritise the subtleties at work behind the mystery of life and its seasonal renewal. In spring snakes rise from the earth, and birds return from the south.

Similarly, the scene we find at Nevali Çori (pictured opposite) was unlikely intended as a literal representation of a snake foraging a corpse. Instead, surely this is a less-differentiated, pre-echo of the Egyptian fire-spitting Uraeus – an extension or psychic efflorescence of the spine-nexus, dorsally complemented in royal regalia by the bull's tail. Are we to similarly understand this snake emerging from a spine-nexus?

The Primordial Twins

We finally turn to the faceless characters of the T-shapes. To date, the imposing pair of stones occupying the outlook of Enclosure D are the oldest megalithic pillars of such scale on our planet. Speculating over the ultimate 'why?' of the T (or Tau) shape would be difficult, since so many varied forms appear over the globe (see, for example, similar structures in Malta). Ignatius Donnelly's remarks on the origin of the shape are however interesting, in light of the age from which Göbekli Tepe hails from:

> In Egypt, Assyria, and Britain it was emblematical of creative power and eternity; in India, China and Scandinavia, of heaven and immortality ... while in both hemispheres it was the common symbol of the resurrection, or 'the sign of the life to come' ... And lastly, we have seen how, as a rule, it is found in conjunction with a stream or streams of water, with exuberant vegetation, and with a hill or mountainous region ... [a place where] Nature, unassisted by man, produces all that is necessary for his sustentation.[16]

Besides parallels with the Egyptian Djed, it would be reasonable to assume the shapes may have derived from items that were of practical use; that they were a glorification of tools. For Sumerians

Snake iconography at Nevali Çori

the chief meteorological deity Enlil, depicted with the hooves and tail of the sacred bull, was said to be responsible for inventing the mattock, an emerging pastoral and building tool which does resemble the T-shapes. Such an association would add credence to the theory that the Sumerians derived from a mother-culture that arrived from the north, said to be of a stature that could even mimic trees in the manner of the druidic god Hu. Perhaps more symbolically though, some of the central T-shapes possess slightly inclining tops, providing them with a semblance of the Egyptian *was*-wand or sceptre, a ritual implement modelled on the penis of the bull as the maker of all things.

The distinctive Tau shape aside, the important central T-shapes of Enclosure D embody what are manifestly two very powerful anthropomorphic beings, both of whom still palpably command an omniscient presence. Who were these strange beings? A mix of exalted ancestor, priest-king and god? Or was there a more specific identity associated with their construction...and if so, are we to consider them related, as siblings, or twins?

Recalling the celestial orientation of Enclosure D, we find both T-shapes facing south – this is purposefully indicated by the position of their arms and loincloths. If standing to the rear, pillar 18 to the left is naturally stationed east, while its twin to the right (pillar 31) is stationed west; both corresponding to where the sun rises and sets each day. At the neck of pillar 18 is a crescent with a punctured disk above that conceivably refers to the sun or to a conspicuous planet such as Venus. While enhancing the twin theme, it would not be unreasonable to assume that the two beaked-beings joined in hand above represent Gemini. Standing just above Orion straddling the Milky Way, this constellation was in Egyptian and earlier Assyrian tradition identified as twins. What is more, this sign was also an important celestial house which could explain the compelling astronomical marks below it. The bull as the moon, on the other hand, forms a medley of related images such as crescents, horns, coils,

Symbols on Pillar 18 of Enclosure D at Göbekli Tepe

and U-signs. Not only was the crescent a major cultic image across Mesopotamia, but even more immediately south of Göbekli Tepe, at Harran. But this was at a time when even the temples of Babylon had become "a heap of ruins, the haunt of jackals, a horror and a hissing, without inhabitant", as reconstructed by Tom Holland:

> ... for in Harran, they still worshipped the ancient gods. The landscape beyond its walls was filled with idols: strangely preserved, withered corpses, both animal and human, were wedged into fissures above mountain roads; eerie figures framed by peacock feathers and crescent moons stood guard over desert lakes. The mightiest idol of all, however, and the glory of Harran itself, was a colossal statue of the city's patron, Sin – the 'Lord of the Moon'.[17]

The crescent moon together with the seven birds moving east-to-west on the base of this pillar, a highly esoteric number in myth and initiation lore, lends this hunter-shaman figure a remarkable

Dionysian/Osirian air. Pillar 31, on the other hand, is marked by a bucranium presided over by a bovine (see opposite). If this was in some way meant to symbolically associate the pillar with Taurus, what associations can we find on its twin? Looking at the detail on pillar 18, if we were to draw a fleeting analogy with the cowboy name-belts of the Wild West, then pehaps the H symbol emblazoned on the belt of the figure (see image on following page of text) is a pictograph of Orion. Importantly, this belt seems to be the 'source' of the sacred H. We note that pillar 31 to the west does not feature this. The bracket-like shapes on either side suggest abstract sails or vectors, as if signifying the H to be floating, or – when there is only one – moving in a direction, like the upturned crescent supporting the disk on the neck of the pillar above. As mentioned earlier, this H emblem plays out a drama on other pillars – it sometimes appears 90° as if 'dead', or signifying an inverted condition. Is there a similarity here with the Djed as the backbone of Osiris/Orion in its alternating straight and tilting appearances, similar to the varying upright-supine positions of the Orion constellation in both its nightly and seasonal wandering over the heavens? The grid or net designs chiseled intricately over several of the pillars suggest that an ancestral 'cosmic hunter' played a large role here. Seeing that the Pleiades are commonly depicted as birds braided or caught in a net, it is suggestive indeed to find seven birds on pillar 12 of Enclosure C moving over a net-like pattern of lines. Whatever species of bird these were intended to depict, they are the same genus as the seven birds at the base of the 'hunter' of Enclosure D.

Peering deep into the Palaeolithic gloom of Lascaux's inner chamber, some 7000 years before Enclosure D's construction, we find a possible clue to the identity of these mysterious T-shaped twins. In her unusual but utterly splendid work *Plato Prehistorian*, Mary Settegast interprets (without over-interpreting) Lascaux's shaft scene in light of the twin mythology of the Magdalenian Golden Age. It is a deeply rooted and widespread cosmogony, with striking counterparts

Bull icon on Pillar 31 of Enclosure D at Göbekli Tepe

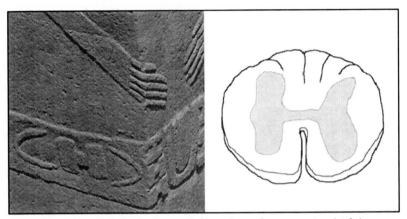

H-symbol on belt of Pillar 18 (left), and spinal cross-section (right)

in Vedic and Scandinavian mythology – which as we have seen may also be integrated into the central T-shapes of Enclosure D at Göbekli Tepe, though patterned differently to the scene at Lascaux. The myth involves the fall from divinity of the god-king Yima, who can be identified with the Vedic Yama, and the Scandinavian giant Ymir, all traceable to the Indo-European root *yemo* – 'twin' – which may relate also to Plato's twin-kings of Atlantis, begotten upon Cleito by Poseidon. These supernatural ancestor twins – the darker of which was sometimes personified as a bull – were amazingly widespread over the ancient world, being found as the divine hero-twins of the Maya, the twin-magicians and builders of megalithic Micronesia Olisihpa and Olsohpa, and the culture-begetting hero twins abroad in Sundaland, home of another site of immense antiquity, Gunung Padang. Closer to home in Sumeria, we find the sky god Anu, father to the Annuna, being twined with Dagan, the chthonic god of fertility and of grain who was said to have held the Pleiades in bondage.

The earliest Iranian source accredits Yima's fall from grace, becoming mortal thereby, to him offering the flesh of cattle to people to eat, which may be connected with the introduction of the institutionalised slaying of the bull replacing more specialised shaman-hunter methods and spirit identity with the beast. Under

Yima's reign both herds and people were said to have increased disproportionately, which meant Yima had to enlarge the world to accommodate them. This perhaps could be seen as symbolising the hunter-gatherer way of life being supplanted by agriculture, a fall anchored by the domestication of the bull more than any other beast.

Settegast finds an analogy in the Lascaux shaft scene with the world-creating death of Yima's ancestor, Gayōmart, and the Primordial Bull.[18] We could perhaps extend this to the representations on Enclosure D's T-shapes of the first man and primordial bull, given the antiquity of the proto-Indo-European – and global – origin-myths involving twins.

If there is something behind the T-shapes at Göbekli Tepe enshrining a conception of the twin-kings, so prevalent across the ancient world as the personification of a Golden Age, then the people of Göbekli Tepe would have been monumentally commemorating their birth, origins, at both the ancestral and cosmic level, with the aim of becoming part of it. To modern onlookers the twins are psychologically rooted in the two hemisphere of the psyche: one rational, ego-assertive; the other in tune with the deeper, unconscious cycles of nature. Sometimes the twins split, become warring and fratricidal, but when in union they are the menhirs of an undivided Eden.

Alistair Coombs is currently writing a PhD on images of fire and light in the Buddhist permutations of consciousness. He is also researching a book on the Pleiades in ancient global cultures.

The DYING LIGHT

Exploring the strange phenomenon of lights seen at the time of death

by *Greg Taylor*

"Sunrise doesn't last all morning, a cloudburst doesn't last all day," sang George Harrison on the title track to his first post-Beatles solo album *All Things Must Pass*. Although the song is naturally seen as an ode to the impermanence of human life, the lyrics also note that never-ending change means that those left grieving can look to the future with hope: "Darkness only stays at night-time, in the morning it will fade away." But Harrison also intimated, through lyrics written in the first-person, that those that die too might move onwards: "None of life's strings can last, so I must be on my way, and face another day".

Three decades after writing this song, the former Beatles guitarist went 'on his way' himself, in the literal sense, dying on the 29th of

November 2001 – aged just 58 – after a battle with lung cancer. Is
it possible that Harrison – a devotee of Indian mysticism – truly
did move on, in some sense, to 'face another day'? Intriguingly, the
extraordinary life of George Harrison seems to have been matched
with an extraordinary death, going by the events his wife Olivia
witnessed as the former Beatle shed this mortal coil:

> There was a profound experience that happened when he left his
> body. It was visible. Let's just say, you wouldn't need to light the
> room, if you were trying to film it. He just…lit the room.[1]

The lazy response to the above testimony would be to mark down
Olivia Harrison's observations as hyperbole – the poetic wish-
fulfilment of a grieving wife – except for the fact that she is far
from alone in witnessing strange phenomena such as this at the
deathbed of loved ones. As I pointed out in my recent book, *Stop
Worrying! There Probably is an Afterlife*,

George Harrison

there have in fact been numerous cases
in which those caring for the dying
have described seeing a bright light
surrounding the dying person, exuding
what they relate as "a raw feeling of
love".[2] And when I say 'numerous', I'm
not exaggerating: neuropsychiatrist Peter
Fenwick was amazed to find in a survey
of palliative carers that *one in every three*
reported accounts of "a radiant light that
envelops the dying person, and may spread throughout the room
and involve the carer", a description which sounds remarkably
similar to the "profound experience" recounted by Olivia
Harrison. In a similar Dutch study, the numbers were even more
staggering: *more than half* of all carers reported observations of
this 'dying light'!

Dipping into these experiences on a case-by-case basis, the phenomenon continues to intrigue. Peter Fenwick was told by one lady that while sitting at her dying husband's bedside there was suddenly "a most brilliant light shining from my husband's chest". The light began to rise toward the ceiling, and she began hearing "the most beautiful music and singing voices", filling her with an overwhelming feeling of joy. At this point, the nurse interrupted with news that her husband had just passed, and the light and the music instantly disappeared, leaving the woman bereft at being left behind, after being shown just the barest of glimpses 'behind the veil'.[3]

Similarly, another woman reported that as she watched her mother pass away...

> ...It was then that I saw her face appeared to be glowing with a gold light. The light began to leave through the top of her head and go towards the ceiling. Looking back to my mother's face I saw that she was no longer breathing.[4]

In a survey of palliative care nurses in Australia, one respondent told how he, another nurse, and the patient's husband saw a blue-white light leave the body of the patient and drift toward the ceiling. "As she died we just noticed like an energy rising from her...sort of a bluey white sort of aura," the nurse explained. "We looked at each other, and the husband was on the other side of the bed and he was looking at us... he saw it as well and he said he thinks that she went to a better place". As is often the case, this experience was transformative for the nurse: "It probably changed the way I felt about people dying and what actually happens after death".[5] In fact, the researcher responsible for the Australian study which uncovered this anecdote, Deborah Morris, was herself originally inspired to investigate strange death-bed experiences by her own experience of seeing the 'dying light'. "There was a young man who had died in the room with his family and I saw an aura coming off him," she recounts. "It was like a mist. I didn't tell anybody for years. I've never seen it again".[6]

This 'mist' or 'vapour' leaving the body is another strange element that is sometimes (though certainly not always) reported during experiences of death-bed light (some describe it as smoke or vapour, others say it resembles the shimmer above a hot road, while some witnesses claim even to have seen it coalesce into a human-type shape). One carer told how she awoke in the darkness of early morning to the sight of "a flame licking the top of the wall against the ceiling" above her dying father's bed. "I saw a plume of smoke rising, like the vapour that rises from a snuffed-out candle, but on a bigger scale... it was being thrown off by a single blade of phosphorus light", the witness recounted. "It hung above Dad's bed, about 18 inches or so long, and was indescribably beautiful...it seemed to express perfect love and peace". She switched on the light to investigate further, but the phenomenon instantly vanished; "the room was the same as always on a November morning, cold and cheerless, with no sound of breathing from Dad's bed. His body was still warm". Another carer told of the profound effect seeing such things can have on one's worldview:

As he died something which is very hard to describe because it was so unexpected and because I had seen nothing like it left up through his body and out of his head. It resembled distinct delicate waves/lines of smoke (smoke is not the right word but I have not got a comparison) and then disappeared. I was the only one to see it. It left me with such a sense of peace and comfort. I don't think that we were particularly close as my sister and I had been sent off to boarding school at an early age.

I do not believe in God. But as to an afterlife I now really do not know what to think.

Well-known near-death experience researcher Raymond Moody –
author of the seminal 1970s book on NDEs, *Life After Life* – relates
a case in his recent book *Glimpses of Eternity* in which a Georgia
doctor saw a "bright glow" coming from a recently-deceased patient,
followed by a mist that "formed over the chest area and hovered
there". The doctor noticed some motion to the 'mist', though he
described it as being as subtle as "water moving within water".
Another interviewee, a hospice psychologist from North Carolina,
told Moody they occasionally had seen lights in the room during
someone's passing, and on two occasions had "seen patients leave
their body in cloud form...I would describe these clouds as a sort of
mist that forms around the head or chest".[7]

Another pioneering researcher of strange phenomena occurring
at the time of death was the late Dr. Robert Crookall. In his 1970
book, *Out-of-the-Body Experiences*, Crookall cites the case of Dr. R.
B. Hout, a physician who encountered both anomalous mist and
light in the room during the death of his aunt.

> My attention was called...to something immediately above the
> physical body, suspended in the atmosphere about two feet above the
> bed. At first I could distinguish nothing more than a vague outline
> of a hazy, fog-like substance. There seemed to be only a mist held
> suspended, motionless. But, as I looked, very gradually there grew
> into my sight a denser, more solid, condensation of this inexplicable
> vapor. Then I was astonished to see definite outlines presenting
> themselves, and soon I saw this fog-like substance was a assuming a
> human form... The eyes were closed as though in tranquil sleep, and
> a luminosity seemed to radiate from the spirit body.[8]

What are to make of these tales? Skeptics of the idea of an afterlife have
generally dismissed such testimony as being hallucinations brought on
by the stress of the moment, or wishful thinking by the grieving. But
how then do we explain the many stories in which *multiple witnesses*

in the same room saw this phenomenon occurring, such as the case mentioned above from the Australian survey of palliative carers, in which two nurses and the patient's husband all saw "a blue-white light leave the body of the patient and drift toward the ceiling"? Peter Fenwick relates an instance in which a person, at the time of their brother's death, witnessed "odd tiny sparks of bright light" emanating from the body – and what's more, these 'sparks' were also seen by another person in the room. In one of Raymond Moody's case files, an entire family witnessed the dying light at their mother's bedside:

> The day my mother died, my two brothers, my sister, my sister-in-law and I were all in the room. My mother hadn't spoken a word in several hours, and she was breathing in an irregular pattern. None of us were really upset because mother had been on a long downhill course and we knew this was the end.
>
> Suddenly, a bright light appeared in the room. My first thought was that a reflection was shining through the window from a vehicle passing by outside. Even as I thought that, however, I knew it wasn't true, because this was not any kind of light on this earth. I nudged my sister to see if she saw it too, and when I looked at her, her eyes were as big as saucers. At the same time I saw my brother literally gasp. Everyone saw it together and for a little while we were frightened.
>
> Then my mother just expired and we all kind of breathed a big sigh of relief.[9]

In another case, a hospice worker named David told how he was "stunned" during the passing of a patient with pancreatic cancer when a bright light filled the room, visible to all those present including the dying woman's husband. He described it as "the brightest light I'd ever seen", though it seemed more like a "plasma or the kind of light you see when you get snow-blinded".

If this 'dying light' is not an hallucination, what could it be? Is it some sort of energy emitted during the physical death of the body that takes visible form? Or is it some sort of 'psychical' manifestation that can only be observed with the mind in a certain state? Is there any relationship between this light seen at deathbeds, and the 'white light' so often witnessed by those who have a near-death experience? At this point, we have a lot of questions, but very few – if any – answers. There are possible ways forward from a scientific point of view – for example, Peter Fenwick has suggested that light sensors could be set up in hospice rooms in an attempt to record increases in the amount of light – but at the end of the day, it seems we will likely always be left to make a judgement call based only on anecdotes, or in some cases our own experiences. One thing is sure though: those who have experienced this 'dying light' for themselves will likely not be swayed by skeptical arguments. For them, like Olivia Harrison, the experience is profoundly meaningful, and the weak 'explanations' of the phenomenon from those who cleave to a skeptical (or perhaps more correctly, materialist) philosophy would bear all the impact of a butterfly trying to move an elephant.

The Bengali poet Rabindrananth Tagore wrote that "Death is not extinguishing the light, it is putting out the lamp because dawn has come". His words seem a lot more literal once we are familiar with accounts of the dying light.

Greg Taylor is the owner and editor of the online alternative news portal, *The Daily Grail* (www.dailygrail.com), and is also the editor of *Darklore*. He is widely read in topics that challenge the orthodox worldview, from alternative history to the mysteries of human consciousness. Greg currently resides in Brisbane, Australia. He has written two guidebooks to the esoteric topics in Dan Brown's novels: *The Guide to Dan Brown's The Lost Symbol* and *Inside Dan Brown's Inferno*. His latest book *Stop Worrying! There Probably is an Afterlife* is an exploration of the evidence for the survival of consciousness after death.

ENDNOTES

Mike Jay - Dreaming While Awake (p. 11)

Acknowledgements:

A version of this piece first appeared in *London Review of Books*, Vol. 35, No. 5, 7 March 2013.

Notes:

1. Oliver Sacks, *Hallucinations* (2012), p.21

2. quoted in German Berrios, *History of Mental Symptoms* (1996), p.37

3. Jacques-Joseph Moreau de Tours, *Hashish and Mental Illness* (1845/tr. 1972), p.165

4. Alfred Maury, *De l'hallucination...* (1845), p.14

5. in Shane McCorristine (ed.), *Spiritualism, Mesmerism and the Occult, Vol. 1* (2012), pp.187-9

6. all *ibid.*, p.208

7. *ibid.*, p. 214

8. Dominic ffytche, Visual Hallucinatory Syndromes: past, present and future, in *Dialogues in Clinical Neuroscience*, v.9 (2), June 2007

9. Terence McKenna, *Time and Mind – The Tykes* (http://www.erowid.org/culture/characters/mckenna_terence/mckenna_terence_time_mind.shtml)

10. http://blogs.scientificamerican.com/cross-check/2012/06/06/was-psychedelic-guru-terence-mckenna-goofing-about-2012-prophecy/

11. Oliver Sacks, *Hallucinations* (2012) pp.108-9

Martin Shough - A Social History of Ball Lightning (p. 27)

Acknowledgements:

This is a revised version of an article originally published in *Magonia*, #81, May 2003.

Notes:

1. Kuiper, G., 'Presentation at Arizona Academy of Science Meeting, Apr. 29 1967', in: Gillmor, D.S. (ed.), *Scientific Study of Unidentified Flying Objects,* Vision Press 1970 pp.839-43.

2. Jones, R.V., "The Natural Philosophy of Flying Saucers", in: Gillmor (ed.), op.cit. pp.922-33.

3. Cade, C.M. & D. Davis, *The Taming of the Thunderbolts,* Abelard-Schuman, London 1969, pp.93-104.

4. Lane, F.W., *The Elements Rage: The Extremes of Natural Violence, Vol. 1,* revised ed., Sphere Books, London 1968 p.141.

5. *Ibid.,* p.121.

6. Klass, P.J., "Plasma Theory May Explain Many UFOs", *Aviation Week & Space Technology,* Aug.22, 1966, p.48.

7. Klass, P.J., "Many UFOs are Identified as Plasmas", *Aviation Week & Space Technology,* Oct.3, 1966, p.54.

8. Klass, P.J., *UFOs Identified,* Random House, NY 1968.

9. Altschuler, M.D., "Atmospheric Electricity and Plasma Interpretations of UFOs", in: Gillmor, D.S. (ed.), op.cit., pp.723-55.

10. See http://martinshough.com/aerialphenomena/Lakenheath/background.htm

11. Altschuler, M.D., 'Atmospheric Electricity and Plasma Interpretations of UFOs', in: Gilmor (Ed.) *Scientific Study of |Unidentified Flying Objects* [Condon Report], Vision Press 1970, p.723; see also, e.g., Cade, C.M. & D. Davis, *The Taming of the Thunderbolts,* Abelard-Schuman, London 1969, p.61; Singer, S., *The Nature of Ball Lightning.* Plenum Press, New York, 1971.

12. Letter to the author. A version of this article first appeared in 2003 in *Magonia* which finally folded in 2009 after thirty years (and another ten under different titles). http://magoniamagazine.blogspot.co.uk/search/label/Magonia%2099

Daniel Bourke - The Book of Death...and Beyond (p. 71)

Notes:

1. Kalweit, *Dreamtime and Inner Space, The World of the Shaman*
2. *Tibetan Book of the Dead (Bardo Thodol)*, p. 12.
3. *Tibetan Book of the Dead (Bardo Thodol)*, p. 20
4. Wilson, *Life after Death: The Evidence*, p. 67.
5. Zuni tribesman to anthropologist Frank Cushing in 1882, as reported by Kalweit in *Dreamtime and Inner Space*, Chapter 4
6. http://dedroidify.blogspot.ie/2008/10/aj-ayer-prominent-skeptics-beliefs.html
7. Moody, *Life after Life*
8. *Tibetan Book of the Dead (Bardo Thodol)*, p. 33.
9. Moody, *Life after Life*, PDF, p. 46.
10. Morse, *Closer to the Light: Learning form the Near Death Experiences as Children*, Chapter 5
11. http://www.nderf.org/NDERF/NDE_Experiences/bolette_l_nde.htm
12. http://www.nderf.org/NDERF/NDE_Experiences/robyn_nde.htm
13. Wilson, *Life after Death: The Evidence*, p. 139.
14. Quoted in R. Noyes and R. Kletti, "Panoramic memory: A response to the threat of death", *Omega, 8*, p. 182.
15. Alexander, *Proof of Heaven*, Chapter 33
16. The NDE of Dr. Arthur Yensen, http://news-beacon-ireland.info/?p=12951
17. http://www.nderf.org/NDERF/NDE_Experiences/lisa_b_nde.htm
18. *Tibetan Book of the Dead (Bardo Thodol)*, p. 36.
19. http://www.nderf.org/NDERF/NDE_Experiences/bolette_l_nde.htm
20. The Near Death Experience of Vicki Umipeg, documented in many books on the subject, http://www.near-death.com/experiences/evidence03.html
21. Ring, *Heading Towards Omega*, pp. 42-43
22. http://www.nderf.org/NDERF/NDE_Experiences/brian_t's_nde.htm
23. Van Lommel, *Consciousness beyond Life: The Science of the Near Death Experience*, P. 23.
24. *Tibetan Book of the Dead (Bardo Thodol)*, p. 36.
25. Three Near-Death Experiences with Premonitions of What Could Have Been", *Journal of Near-Death Studies*, Spring 1991, p.191
26. Quoted from Ian Wilson, *Life after Death: The Evidence*, Notes and References, p. 263., Sabom, op.cit, p. 34. (The confusing nature of this entry is due to the fact

that I do not own this particular book myself)

27. Quoted by Kalweit, *Dreamtime and Inner Space-The World of the Shaman*, p. 53.

28. Six Studies of Out-of-the-Body Experiences, Charles T. Tart,

29. *Tibetan Book of the Dead (Bardo Thodol)*, p. 9.

30. Moody, op.cit, p. 39

31. Chris Carter, *Science and the Near Death Experience*, p. 99

32. Carter, op.cit, p. 94.

33. Sabom, op.cit. p. 53.

34. Moody, op.cit, p. 36

35. Sutherland, *Transformed by the Light*, New York and London, Bantam, 1992, p. 6.)

36. Wilson op.cit p. 139

37. *Tibetan Book of the Dead (Bardo Thodol)*, p. 39.

38. http://www.nderf.org/NDERF/NDE_Experiences/samantha_h_nde.htm

39. Wilson op.cit p. 146

40. Wilson op.cit p. 148

41. Moody, op.cit, p. 35

42. Quoted in Melvin Morse, *Parting Visions: An Exploration of Pre-Death Psychic and Spiritual Experiences*, London, Pliatkus, 1995, pp. 104-5

Ian 'Cat' Vincent - Believing in Fiction (p. 93)

Notes:

1. http://tinyurl.com/kjvdxbu

2. It should be noted Possamai's term is not the only one in the field: other terms such as 'The Postmodern Sacred' (coined by Emily McAvan in her book of the same name, McFarland, 2012) and the pleasingly direct 'Invented Religions' (by Carole Cusack in *Invented Religions: Imagination, Fiction and Faith*, Ashgate, 2010) exist.

3. *Religion And Popular Culture: A Hyper-Real Testament* by Adam Possamai (Gods, Humans and Religions No. 7, P.I.E, Peter Lang 2007), ISSN 1377-8323

4. *Handbook of Hyper-real Religions*, ed. Adam Possamai (Brill Handbooks on Contemporary Religion, vol. 5, Brill 2012), ISSN 1874-6691

5. Possamai, *Handbook of Hyper-Real Religions*, p.1

6. *Simulacres et Simulation*, 1981 - English translation 1984.

7. Umberto Eco, *Travels In Hyperreality*, New York, Harcourt Brace Jovanovich, 1986

8. 'Late Capitalism' was coined by Wehner Sombart (1863-1041) in his *Der Moderne Kapitalismus* (1902); the modern usage mostly comes from the work of Frederic Jameson (1934-) and his students, as a result of his influential work *Postmodernism, or, The Cultural Logic of Late Capitalism*. Other thinkers, such as Jacques Derrida, prefer terms such as neo-capitalism or post-capitalism.

9. I talk in greater depth about this – especially its similarity to the concept of Cargo Cults – in my earlier look at Possamai's work in the article 'Into The Hyper-Real', published in *Apocalyptic Imaginary* (ed. James Curcio, Mythos Media 2012, ISBN-13: 978-0615590011) pp. 114-17

10. This is caused in part, I believe, by people unable to deal with both this loss of certainty in traditional structures and the information overload which come with the wider availability of alternative narratives, who then fall into a reflex fundamentalism of belief. This can be seen as a manifestation of what Alvin Toffler called 'Future Shock' in his book of that name (Random House, 1970, ISBN 0-394-42586-3) - I've always preferred the later version of the term, 'going futzy', from the comic *Judge Dredd*.

11. Possamai, *A Hyper-Real Testament*, p.48.

12. There are ample scientific studies on how human minds work so thoroughly with narrative structures: some good layman-level entry points on this can be found in pieces such as 'Favorite TV reruns may have restorative powers' (http://tinyurl.com/994zoeb) and "Losing Yourself" In A Fictional Character Can Affect Your Real Life' (http://tinyurl.com/7mfolrz). An interesting recent study can be seen here: http://tinyurl.com/lwbjjrr

13. Much has been written about Hubbard, Parsons and the Agape Lodge of the OTO. A very enjoyable fictional retelling of this saga can be found in Jake Arnott's novel *The House Of Rumour* (Sceptre, 2012, ISBN-13: 978-0340922729)

14. Puttnam 1961, ISBN 978-0-441-79034-0. It should be noted that one aspect of the water-sharing ritual in the novel – that of consensual cannibalism – was never part of the CAW's praxis!

15. I have written in depth about my experience of IDIC as a belief in the article 'Infinite Diversity' for Modern Mythology: http://tinyurl.com/menzkwr

16. Knopf, 1983, ISBN 0-394-52406-3

17. *The Way of Wyrd: Tales of an Anglo-Saxon Sorcerer* (Century, 1983, ISBN 978-0-7126-0277-8)

18. Of course, a case can be made that neo-paganism has always drawn on mostly invented sources, specifically the overly-romanticized Victorian interpretation of Celtic and 'druidical' mythology. The work of Professor Ronald Hutton is especially illuminating in this regard.

19. Muller 1972, ISBN 0-87728-217-X

20. *The Necronomicon: The Book Of Dead Names*, edited by George Hay, Corgi, 1978, ISBN 1871438160. The curious can find a set of extracts of the alleged original text of that version of the tome here: http://tinyurl.com/msj4b8x

21. Including the excellent comedy/horror/SF/urban magic Laundry Files Series by Charles Stross - start with *The Atrocity Archives* (Ace, 2006, ISBN 0441013651)

22. One especially controversial series of comics by writer/magician Alan Moore (*The Courtyard, Neonomicon* and an upcoming third book in the series which directly deals with Lovecraft's life) make the sexual undertones Lovecraft eschewed graphically explicit, including several rape scenes.

23. Possamai, op. cit., p. 88

24. Atria Books, 2006, ISBN 978-1-58270-170-7 – and a worse example of the Pollyanna-minded, privileged, genuine-occult-praxis-corrupting wish-fulfilment aspects of New Age spirituality would be hard to find.

25. Possamai notes (op. cit., pp 130-31) that the lineage of the majority of the New Age movement can be traced back to the earlier drawing of Eastern myths into the West via the Theosophical Society. Although this was an undoubted influence on all later pop mysticism, the commercial aspect did not truly rear its head until the 1960-70's.

26. Possamai, op. cit., pp.49-50. Possamai later examines the area of cultural exploitation and appropriation by the New Age sector, but this discussion is beyond the scope of the current article.

27. Possamai, op. cit., pp.48-9.

28. Possamai, op. cit., p.51

29. Possamai, op. cit., p.52

30. Joseph Campbell, *The Hero Of A Thousand Faces*, Pantheon 1949, ISBN 978-1-57731-593-3

31. Interview with George Lucas http://www.next-wave.org/may99/starwars.htm, cited in Possamai, op. cit., p.75

32. Possamai (op. cit., p.72) cites a figure of 70,509 people in Australia. The official UK figure was 390,127. There was however a sizeable fall in the 2011 census: UK Jedi numbered 176,632 and fell to seventh place among religions, behind Judaism and Hinduism. See http://tinyurl.com/af889kn. I discussed the 2011 census and the atheist backlash against the Jedi in *Apocalyptic Imaginary*, pp110-13.

33. http://www.orderofthejedi.org

34. http://tinyurl.com/ldfq7es

35. http://www.theregister.co.uk/2006/11/16/jedi_petition/

36. http://news.bbc.co.uk/1/hi/scotland/glasgow_and_west/8003067.stm

37. I explored the legal and moral ramifications of this event in the article "...Of Jedi and Jail" here: http://www.catvincent.com/?page_id=776. As there, I would note that there are plenty of canonical examples of Jedi lowering their hood in public...

38. http://tinyurl.com/c27auc. It should be noted, however, that a 2011 UK Supreme Court case brought by two Scientologists led to a ruling that belief in a supreme deity was not a necessary aspect for a religion to receive recognition and legal rights. See http://tinyurl.com/mapc4vk.

39. Baudrillard often insisted that Disneyland was the perfect simulation of the idealised American town.

40. Fnord.

41. I have touched on the subject of the Otherkin in an earlier piece, here: http://www.catvincent.com/?page_id=773. To date, there has only been one published work specifically on the subject of Otherkin – *A Field Guide To Otherkin* (Megalithica, 2007, ISBN-10: 190571307X) – but it should be noted that its author Lupa has both repudiated her identification as Otherkin and the majority of that work. More information on their beliefs can be found at otherkin.net

42. *Six-Gun Gorilla* is a comic book created by Simon Spurrier and Jeff Stokely (Boom! Studios, 2013), which deals directly with the intervention of the fictional into the comics' quotidian reality. An interesting read.

43. A fine collection of Jack Chick tomes can be found at http://www.monsterwax. com/chick.html. Of course, parodies of Chick's work have also appeared, the best known being the Pagan-oriented comic *Saturnalia* (http://e-sheep.sansara.net.ua/ www.e-sheep.com/Saturnalia/).

44. Compass Books, 2006. ISBN-13: 978-0976196624

45. I discuss Moore and Idea-Space in some depth in my consideration of another manifestation of the avowedly fictional into the world, in the *Darklore* Volume 7 piece "Killing Slenderman".

46. A detailed look at this from a lawyers' perspective can be found in the article 'CSI and the Threshold of Guilt: Managing Truth and Justice in Reality and Fiction' by Tom R. Tyler in The Yale Law Journal http://www.yalelawjournal.org/ pdf/115-5/Tyler.pdf

47. http://abcnews.go.com/US/wireStory/12-year-wisconsin-girls-stab-friend-19-times-23959855

48. http://copycateffect.blogspot.co.uk/2014/06/slenderman2.html

49. I discuss Slenderman in the context of the hyper-real in my article in *Fortean Times* (issue 317).

50. In his book of that name (Red Wheel/Weiser, 2007). Knowles is a proponent of the highly hyper-real practice of synchromysticism – drawing on pop culture

as a manifestation of synchronicity. More of his fascinating writing on the subject can be found at secretsun.blogspot.com

Lucy Ryder - *Walking in the Shadow of Death* (p. 139)

Acknowledgements:

An earlier version of this article first appeared in *The Famulus*.

Notes:

1. Astill, G. 1988 Rural Settlement: the Toft and the Croft. In G. Astill and A. Grant (eds.) *The Countryside of Medieval England*. Oxford. Routledge. p. 36.

2. Devereux, P. 2003. *Spirit Roads: An Exploration of Otherworldly Routes*. London: Collins & Brown. pp. 25-27.

3. 1860. *Notes and Queries for Readers and Writers, Collectors and Librarians: A Medium of Inter-communication for Literary Men, Artists, Antiquaries, Genealogists, Etc,* Third series Volume 9. London: Bell & Daldy

4. Roud, S. 2010. *London Lore: The legends and traditions of the world's most vibrant city*. London: Arrow. p. 167.

5. Ackermann, A. S. E. 1970. *Popular fallacies: A book of common errors: explained and corrected with copious references to authorities*. Detroit: Gale Research Co. p. 466.

6. Hall Cane, Sir. 1887. *A Son of Hagar: A Romance of our Time*. Library of Alexandria

7. Rollinson, W. 1981. *Life & tradition in the Lake District*. London: M Dent & Sons Ltd. p. 69.

8. Brand, J, Ellis, H, Orchard Halliwell-Phillipps, J. 1849. *Observations on the popular antiquities of Great Britain: chiefly illustrating the origin of our vulgar and provincial customs, ceremonies, and superstitions,* Volume 2. London: Henry G Bohn. p. 203.

9. 1871. *Notes and Queries for Readers and Writers, Collectors and Librarians: A Medium of Inter-communication for Literary Men, Artists, Antiquaries, Genealogists, Etc,* Fourth series Volume 8. London: Bell & Daldy.

10. Hillaby, J. 1982. Dirge for the Dead. *New Scientist* 25 February. p. 529.

11. Briggs, K. 2002. *The Fairies in Tradition and Literature*. London: Routledge.

12. Scott, W. 1833. *The Complete Works of Sir Walter Scott with a Biography and his last additions and Illustrations in Seven Volumes*. Volume 4. New York: Conner & Cooke. pp. 73-6.

13. Devereux, 2003. p. 49.

Ray Grasse - Portals of Strangeness (p. 153)

Notes:

1. My thanks to Jessica Hines for her perspective on the incident with the Egyptian statue.

2. The closeness of the protest march on Washington to the Patterson-Gimlin incident one day earlier first came to my attention through Loren Coleman, a well-known cryptozoologist with a keen eye for synchronistic patterns.

Robert M. Schoch - Life, Death, and Raymond (p. 189)

Notes:

1. See: Robert M. Schoch and Logan Yonavjak, editors and compilers. *The Parapsychology Revolution: A Concise Anthology of Paranormal and Psychical Research.* New York: Jeremy P. Tarcher/Penguin, 2008.

2. Sir Olivier Lodge. *The Survival of Man: A Study in Unrecognized Human Faculty.* New York: Moffat, Yard and Company, 1909.

3. Sir Oliver J. Lodge, *Raymond, or Life and Death*, fourth edition. London: Methuen & Company, 1916.

4. See Lodge 1916 [note 3].

5. Here I (Robert Schoch) would note that Lodge is presumably referring to telepathy between discarnate non-material entities and living humans during a séance or in other situations, as human-to-human telepathy could be using the brains of the persons involved (or possibly other bodily organs).

6. Lodge 1916 [note 3], p. 313; material in brackets inserted by R. Schoch.

7. Stuart Hameroff and Deepak Chopra. Chapter 5, "The 'Quantum Soul': A Scientific Hypothesis", *in* A. Moreira-Almeida and F. S. Santos, editors. *Exploring Frontiers of the Mind-Brain Relationship,* Mindfulness in Behavioral Health. Springer Science + Business Media, 2012, pp. 79-93; quotation from p. 80; their references removed from the quotation.

8. Michel Bitbol. "Is Consciousness primary?" *NeuroQuantology*, vol. 6, no. 1, pp. 53-72, 2008; version accessed and consulted was downloaded from the Internet (http://philsci-archive.pitt.edu/4007/1/ConsciousnessPrimaryArt2.pdf) on 6 February 2014 with pagination of 1- 21; quotation from, p. 14.

9. Hameroff and Chopra 2012 [note 7], p. 80.

10. Bitbol 2008 [note 8], p. 16; italics in the original.

11. Stuart Hameroff and Roger Penrose. "Consciousness in the universe: A review of the 'Orch OR' theory." *Physics of Life Reviews*, 2013, Elsevier B.V. http://dx.doi.org/10.1016/j.plrev.2013.08.002, 40 pages; quotation from p. 2, italics in the original.

12. John G. Cramer. Chapter 9 "The Plane of the Present and the New Transactional Paradigm of Time", *in* Robin Drurie, editor. *Time and the Instant.* Clinamen Press, UK, 2001. See also: Robert M. Schoch. *Forgotten Civilization: The Role of Solar Outbursts in Our Past and Future.* Rochester, Vermont: Inner Traditions, 2012, pp. 247-248.

13. See Hameroff and Chopra 2012 [note 7], p. 82.

14. Hugh Everett, III. "'Relative State' Formulation of Quantum Mechanics", *Reviews of Modern Physics*, vol. 29, no. 3, July 1957. Available at http://www.univer.omsk.su/omsk/Sci/Everett/paper1957.html Accessed 12 February 2014.

15. Wojciech H. Zurek. "Decoherence and the Transition from Quantum to Classical—*Revisited*", *Los Alamos Science,* Number 27 (2002), pp. 2-25; quotation from p. 5; material in brackets added by R. Schoch.

16. Hameroff and Chopra 2012 [note 7], p. 82.

17. Hameroff and Chopra 2012 [note 7], p. 83.

18. Hameroff and Chopra 2012 [note 7], p. 83.

19. Hameroff and Penrose 2013 [note 11], p. 11; material in brackets added by R. Schoch.

20. Hameroff and Chopra 2012 [note 7], p. 83; material in brackets added by R. Schoch.

21. Hameroff and Penrose 2013 [note 11].

22. Hameroff and Penrose 2013 [note 11], p. 13.

23. Hameroff and Penrose 2013 [note 11], p. 14.

24. Hameroff and Penrose 2013 [note 11], p. 3.

25. Hameroff and Penrose 2013 [note 11], p. 34.

26. Hameroff and Chopra, 2012 [note 7], p. 90; material in brackets added by R. Schoch.

27. The concept that the universe is essentially a hologram, where the commonly understood structure of space-time is in fact an emergent property of information that can be visualized as stored on a surface or screen that wraps around the universe, is not incompatible with the ideas put forth here. It may be through the "mechanism" of such a holographic concept that consciousness collectively has shaped a relatively agreed upon and consistent universe. For further thoughts on a holographic conception of the universe, see: Robert M. Schoch. "Moving the Moai", *Darklore*, vol. 5 (2010), pp. 134-155, 268-270.

28. See, for instance: Rupert Sheldrake. "Part I: Mind, Memory, and Archetype: Morphic Resonance and the Collective Unconscious", *Psychological Perspectives,* 1987[?]. Available from http://www.sheldrake.org/files/pdfs/papers/morphic1_paper. pdf Accessed 12 February 2014; Rupert Sheldrake. "Society, Spirit & Ritual: Morphic Resonance and the Collective Unconscious - Part II", *Psychological Perspectives,* vol. 18, no. 2 (Fall 1987), pp. 320-331. Available from http://www.sheldrake.org/files/ pdfs/papers/morphic2_paper.pdf Accessed 12 February 2014; Rupert Sheldrake. "Society, Spirit & Ritual: Morphic Resonance and the Collective Unconscious Part III", Available from http://www.sheldrake.org/files/pdfs/papers/morphic3_paper.pdf Accessed 12 February 2014.

29. Imogen Clarke. "Looking beyond the 'modernists': Sir Oliver Lodge and the public face of 1920s physics", article posted at http://www.oliverlodge.org/; posted 22 January 2014. Accessed 10 February 2014.

30. John 1:1 (*The Jerusalem Bible,* With Abridged Introductions and Notes. Alexander Jones, general editor. London: Darton, Longman and Todd, 1968).

Alistair Coombs - Cult of the Cosmic Bull (p. 215)

Notes:

1. Fred Wendorf & Romauld Schild "Nabta Playa and Its Role in Northeastern African Prehistory" in *Journal of Anthropological Archaeology* 17, 1998 pp. 99-101

2. Robert Bauval and Thomas Brophy *Black Genesis: The Prehistoric Origins of Ancient Egypt.* Rochester, Vt.: Bear & Company, 2011 p. 262

3. Michael Brass "Tracing the Origins of the Ancient Egyptian Cattle Cult" in *A Delta Man in Yebu* (ed.) Eyma, A.K. and Bennett, C.J. Universal-Publishers, 2003 pp. 102-5

4. While not mentioning the Pleiades, Naydler provides insightful analysis of the Khoiak festival – Jeremy Naydler *Temple of the Cosmos.* Rochester, Vt.: Inner Traditions 1996 pp. 78-84

5. Calvin W. Schwabe, Joyce Adams and Carleton T. Hodge "Egyptian Beliefs about the Bull's Spine: An Anatomical Origin for Ankh" in *Anthropological Linguistics* Vol.24, No.4 1982 pp. 445-479

6. R.O. Faulkner (trans.) *The Ancient Egyptian Pyramid Texts.* Warminster: Aris & Philips, 1993 p. 100 – Utterance 318

7. Variant of CT Spell 407 cited in Schwabe C, et al (1982) p. 448

8. R.O. Faulkner (trans.) *The Ancient Egyptian Coffin Texts.* Vol.2 Spells 355-787. Warminster: Aris & Philips 1994 p. 257 – Spell 691

9. R.O. Faulkner (trans.) *The Ancient Egyptian Book of the Dead*. London: British Museum Press, 1996 p. 144 – Spell 149

10. Giorgio de Santillana and H. von Dechend *Hamlet's Mill*. Boston: David R. Godine 1977 pp. 124-25. In Siberian shamanism, however, the drum is produced from a variety of animal hides.

11. Robert M. Schoch, PhD, *Forgotten Civilisation*. Rochester, Vt.: Inner Traditions 2012 pp. 53-56

12. See http://en.wikipedia.org/wiki/Axial_precession for a more detailed explanation.

13. Oliver Dietrich, Manfred Heun, Jens Notroff, Klaus Schmidt & Martin Zarnkow "The role of cult and feasting in the emergence of Neolithic communities. New evidence from Göbekli Tepe, south-eastern Turkey" in *ANTIQUITY* 86, 2012 p. 690

14. Klaus Schmidt "Göbekli Tepe – the Stone Age Sanctuaries. New results of ongoing excavations with a special focus on sculptures and high reliefs" in *Documenta Praehistorica* XXXVII, 2010 pp. 242-43 (http://arheologija.ff.uni lj.si/documenta/authors37/37_21.pdf)

15. Joris Peters and Klaus Schmidt "Animals in the symbolic world of Pre-Pottery Neolithic Göbekli Tepe, south-eastern Turkey: a preliminary assessment" in *Anthropozoologica* 39 (1) 2004 p. 208 (http://www.mnhn.fr/museum/front/medias/publication/10613 Peters.pdf)

16. Ignatius Donnelly *Atlantis: The Antediluvian World*. New York: Dover 1976 pp. 321-22

17. Tom Holland *In the Shadow of the Sword: The Battle for Global Empire and the End of the Ancient World*. London: Little Brown Book Group 2012 pp. 107-108

18. Mary Settegast *Plato Prehistorian: 10,000 to 5000 B.C. in Myth and Archaeology*. Cambridge, Mass: Rotenberg Press 1987 pp. 106-10

Greg Taylor - The Dying Light (p. 243)

Acknowledgements:

This essay was originally published in *The Heretic Magazine*, edited by Andrew Gough.

Notes:

1. *Living in the Material World* documentary, directed by Martin Scorcese.
2. Fenwick, Peter. "Dying: A Spiritual Experience as Shown by Near Death

Experiences and Deathbed Visions". http://goo.gl/YcmzuQ

3. Fenwick, P. B. C., and Elizabeth Fenwick. *The art of dying.* Bloomsbury Academic, 2008

4. O'Connor, Deborah. "Palliative Care Nurses' Experiences of Paranormal Phenomena and Their Influence on Nursing Practice", unpublished conference paper.

5. Santos, Franklin Santana, and Peter Fenwick. "Death, End of Life Experiences, and Their Theoretical and Clinical Implications for the Mind–Brain Relationship." In *Exploring Frontiers of the Mind-Brain Relationship*, pp. 165-189. Springer New York, 2012

6. 'The Death Whisperers", *The Weekend Australian*, http://goo.gl/JXNjrs

7. *Glimpses of Eternity*, Raymond Moody and Paul Perry

8. Cited at http://whitecrowbooks.com/michaeltymn/entry/strange_deathbed_mist_light_explained

9. *Glimpses of Eternity*, Raymond Moody and Paul Perry

CPSIA information can be obtained at www.ICGtesting.com
Printed in the USA
BVOW05s2035100914

366213BV00003B/570/P